# UNBROKEN
## GENERATIONAL CURSES

*How To Be Set Free*

Dr. Deborah Pople-Smith

# Copyrights



ISBN: 9798841657446

Publisher: Inspire Publishing, The Bahamas

www.Inspirepublishing.org

Cover Design: Teri M. Bethel

Author Contact:

Dr. Deborah Pople-Smith

P. O. Box F-44355, Freeport,

Grand Bahama, The Bahamas

Email: pople.smith1962@gmail.com

# Dedication

To Dollie Christine & Baldwin Roscoe

# ACKNOWLEDGMENTS

To The Father, Son, and Holy Spirit, who is the head of my life. All wisdom, power, and glory to my God.

With gratitude to my wonderful husband Baldwin, your love, friendship, and partnership have made an immeasurable difference in my life. Thank you for your patience, words of encouragement, support, and prayers during those challenging moments.

Thanks To:

My children: Delisa, Rudolph Jr., Moniqua, Reginald, Ruth, and Dwayne; I am grateful for your words of encouragement, support, and prayers.

Pastor Dr. Jeffrey K. Thompson and Pastor Sidney Pinder JP; for your prayers, assistance, and guidance throughout my studies.

Glenda Williams and Denise Thompson, who constantly prayed, encouraged, and supported me when I needed them most. Also, Audreyanna Clarke, Gilda Saunders, Kathleen Guinea, Perrylyn Hall, Meredith Atwood, Luann Eulin, Susan, Margaritta, Jule, Troy, and Samuel Culmer. Patrice Carey, Debra Miller, Rufus, Kendal, Jonathan, and Garnet Pople; I am forever grateful.

Dr. James H. Vick II (Jacksonville Theological Seminary), Bishop Wellington A. Williams Esq., Minister Teresita Jones, Christian Counselor & Minister of Music Rudolph McKinney Jr., Minister Simone Hutson, Dr. Christine Higgs, and Minister Mary Russell; for your direct and indirect contributions to this book.

I am thankful for the articles by Minister Kevin Ewing, Pastor Jake Kail, Pastor Hank Hanegraaff, Madeline Adams, and Meg Bucher. Also, for the writings of Don Nori, Smith Wigglesworth, Adolf Hitler, Shane W. Houle, Rebecca Brown, and Daniel Yoder.

**Please note:** The information used in this book is written in its original form and may contain grammatical errors, according to grammar rules. Also, quotes from Minister Kevin Ewing were paraphrased.

# REVIEWS

Dr. Deborah Pople-Smith indisputably co-labored with the Holy Spirit to produce a profound, scripture-based, revelatory work. Unbroken Generational Curses How to be set free, is teeming with wisdom nuggets and strategies, which are crucial for Christians and unbelievers to break stubborn barriers to their breakthroughs. This page-turner presents potential readers with a mirror that exposes how vulnerable we are without the protection of the blood of Jesus Christ and the acceptance of the gift of salvation. As the layers of revelation are uncovered, thought-provoking truths become strikingly evident. We come face to face with the undeniable notion that we might have become susceptible to curses due to the intentional or unwitting actions of those in our lineage.

The literature presents a candid, well-supported response to the age-old question: Why do bad things happen to good people? The answer proposed might be one of the few plausible reasons yet. Readers are nudged to consider the possibility of ancestral covenants, ownership of ill-fated property, besetting habits, poor choices, and other vices that could have opened doors to the consequences of curses.

The insightful contents equip readers with the strategies to walk in deliverance and freedom from all debilitating curses.

We are challenged to reach for this freedom by means of repentance, Christian counseling, fasting, and praying. Unbroken Generational Curses How to be set free, is undoubtedly an urgent summon to action for all who desire to stand fast in the liberty wherewith Christ hath made us free (Galatians 5:1).

Simone Hutson

Youth Minister, Author, Educator


Over the years, much has been said about generational curses. The big question is, what are generational curses and how do we break them? This book is an instrument to identify these curses and how they can be broken.

We were made in God's likeness, in His image, and we are vessels of honor to bring glory to His name. However, some strongholds still hover over God's people which must be broken. Only then, they will be able to complete the assignments on the earth, that God has given to them.

Much prayer and fasting have been done before this book was written. I sincerely pray that the readers of this book will now be able to identify generational curses and break them from over their lives.

Minister Mary Russell

Freeport, Bahamas.

# TABLE OF CONTENTS

# FOREWORD

Generational curses as we know them are initiated curses by mankind, which have been transferred from one generation to another, and will continue throughout generations until they are broken.

So many people are interested in knowing how to break a curse or generational curses, but I firmly believe that nothing needs to be addressed if it does not exist.

As I recall in Hosea 4:6 how generational curses are initiated, manifested, and can be sustained when one forgets God, He not only forgets them but also their children.

Dr. Deborah Pople-Smith has persevered tremendously and has found it necessary, to bring about the much-needed transparency on this significant topic. Because of much prayer, meditation, and spiritual deliberations; she eagerly awaits the blessings and breakthroughs of many, as they endeavor to read and get into the deep riches of this revelation.

I personally wish to salute Dr. Pople-Smith for her integrity, tenacious spirit, courage, and exuberance to confront unrighteousness. Also, to ably pen the biblical perspectives on both preventative actions and solutions, as it relates to generational curses to the conurbations of the earth. God's continuous blessings are extended to her and her family.

Bishop: Wellington A Williams. Esq.

# PREFACE

*"Beloved, I wish above all things that thou
mayest prosper and be in health, even as thy
soul prospereth. For I rejoiced greatly, when
the brethren came and testified of the truth
that is in thee, even as thou walkest in the truth."
~3 John 2-3*

This book aims to bring creditable sources together, to find out the truth about generational curses, and how to be set free. Persons who participated in providing information for this book, were asked to address several critical questions such as: Do generational curses really exist? Or are they a myth? If they do exist, how can these generational curses be broken? Those persons shared their perspectives via face-to-face and telephone interviews. Articles from several blogs, websites, books, newspapers, and the Bible, were also used to bring clarity to these timely questions.

Information collected from various sources proves that generational curses do exist! It also gives a clear understanding of what generational curses are, how they came about, how they can impact individuals' lives, and how they can be passed down in bloodlines. However, the Bible tells us that God has given the body of Christ, the power and authority to break generational curses; so that individuals and families can be set free from these bondages.

# INTRODUCTION

I live in a country where Christianity is the religion commonly practiced throughout our archipelago. For most of my life, I would hear older persons in various communities, make strange comments about certain individuals or families, whom they suspected lived under some sort of a generational curse or curses. The stigma of generational curses was commonly attached to families where substance abuse or alcoholism was evident, and where young girls had a child or children out of wedlock. Also, in families who experienced a considerable number of tragedies in their lives, and where individuals mysteriously came down with a strange illness or died, when they reached a certain age.

As I got older, I began asking more direct questions concerning generational curses to suffice my curiosity. I noticed that individuals would shy away from my questions or change the subject altogether. I also found it strange that pastors and other ministers in the local church, never spoke about these curses, nor did they address this topic on the pulpit. At that time, I did not realize that discussing generational curses was considered "taboo". I became very curious regarding the fact that only certain families in the community, were suspected of living under a generational curse or curses. I often wondered if those accusations were true or if they were a myth.

# A Testimony

*"And they overcame him by the blood of the
Lamb, and by the word of their testimony."
~Revelation 12:11*

Nearly five years ago, a very dear family member who was the matriarch of her household became dysfunctional, disorientated, and emaciated. She either forgot to eat foods and drink fluids or flat-out refused them. She became paranoid, had episodes of hallucinations, and was convinced that persons were trying to harm or kill her; for her, this was very real. During these episodes, her heart rate and pulse rate would increase tremendously, as her eyes bulged in terror. Trying to run away and escape from her horrors became a routine.

Therefore, security screened windows and double bolted doors, had to be installed, and properly secured at all times to keep her safe. She lost sense of the time of day, and at intervals, her environment would appear to become a strange place. At this time, she was unable to care for herself, her children, or their home. Her vertical body structure had changed, as she tilted to one side when she stood up, walked, or tried to run away.

Her children were bewildered and questioned her state of mind and deteriorating health. This individual was taken to the hospital for investigations and medical intervention. After running several tests and completing a comprehensive examination, she was diagnosed with Alzheimer's. Medications that were prescribed and given, did not help her ailment because she usually refused to take them, or spat them out of her mouth. The family was told to take her home, give her whatever she wanted to eat or drink, and make her as comfortable as possible.

When the sole provider of a family is reduced to a confused frame of skin and bones; it leaves a family in great despair with so many questions, and so little, or no answers at all. After the initial shock, her children and grandchildren remembered that she taught them the Word of God. Her life's testimony was that God is a provider, a deliverer, and a healer. Also, He is faithful, and will never leave or forsake His children; especially, in times of trouble. You see! She served God for a long time, and He never forsook her in the past, nor did He forsake her family. Therefore, they began to seek the Lord in prayer. As they prayed continuously, the Holy Spirit prompted them to fast and pray on her behalf.

> *"And he said unto them, This kind can come*
> *forth by nothing, but by prayer and fasting."*
> *~Mark 9:29.*

Her children were reminded that because Adam and Eve sinned, this caused curses to be passed down to all humans throughout the generations. Hence, their loved one was not exempt. Her children and grandchildren went down in prayer before the Lord and repented for the sins committed by their ancestors and their sins as well. After constant prayer and fasting, that dear family member arose out of bed one Tuesday afternoon and said, "I am hungry, can I get something to eat please?" As she began to eat and drink a little, the family began to ring on the prayer bells of heaven more than ever before. That loved one's body structure returned to its original form, and she stood upright again. Praise the Lord! Flesh returned to her bones, and she began to fill out. As time passed, she began to walk around her bedroom and later around the house. During the worship hour, it was evident that God had restored her melodious alto voice, as it rang out when she participated in singing the songs of Zion.

Today, her Spirit-Man is strong. She recites the Psalms without hesitation, or a mistake, including her favorite: Psalms 130:1-8. She can bathe herself with assistance and when she insists, she is allowed to wash a few cups and dishes as well. If one were to go to her bedroom door and listen, he or she would hear her talking to the Lord in prayer or singing a familiar chorus. God has truly delivered her through the love and support of her family. Nevertheless, the chains of generational curses were broken through repentance for their sins and the sins of their ancestors. Also, through intense prayer, fasting, casting out evil sick spirits, pulling down ancient and present strongholds, and the intervention of the Holy Spirit. There is power in the name of Jesus! We give God all the glory and honor, which is due to His Holy Name!

*"When the Word and Spirit come together,
there will be the biggest movement of the
Holy Spirit that the nation, and indeed the
world, has ever seen."[1] ~Smith Wigglesworth*

With much research and help from hardworking and dedicated individuals, the truth is revealed. Do generational curses really exist? Or are they a myth? Hang tight, you are about to find out.

# CHAPTER ONE

## What are Generational Curses?

*"And ye shall know the truth, and the truth
shall make you free." ~John 8:32*

For far too long the reality of generational curses has been circumvented and dismissed; as individuals laid back and allowed the enemy to destroy their families, their futures, communities, churches, and the nation at large. The time has come to take back what the enemy has stolen; it is time to protect ourselves, our children, and our future generations.

According to the Collins English Dictionary, the meaning of the word "Generational" when used as an adjective-noun, relates to a particular generation or the relationship between particular generations. The meaning of the word "Curse" when used as a countable noun is: If you say that there is a curse on someone, you mean that there seems to be a supernatural power causing unpleasant things to happen to them.[1]

When both words "Generational Curse" are used together, they imply that there is a supernatural power that causes unpleasant things to happen to a particular generation, or the relationship between particular generations.

Kail states, "A generational curse is an example of a root beneath the surface, which produces bad fruit above the surface. It is simply a curse that is passed down from one generation to the next. Just like we receive an inheritance of physical traits from our parents, we also receive a spiritual inheritance from our family line. This includes both blessings and curses. One of the foundational Scriptures for this is Exodus 20:4-6. "You shall not make for yourself a carved image - any likeness of anything that is in heaven above, or that is in the earth beneath, or that is in the water under the earth; you shall not bow down to them nor serve them. For I, the Lord your God, am a jealous God, visiting the iniquity of the fathers upon the children to the third and fourth generations of those who hate Me, but showing mercy to thousands, to those who love Me and keep My commandments." The iniquity of parents is visited upon their children."[2]

Kail used an example of a tree root beneath the surface of the earth, which produces bad fruit above the surface; to bring awareness of how generational curses can thrive, as they lay dormant in the lives of individuals. Eventually, these curses become evident by creating havoc in one way or the other. Interestingly, fifty percent of a tree is underground in the form of roots. Roots are important for the health and longevity of a tree. They search for nutrients and water, serve as a conduit for nutrients and store them. Roots also provide anchorage for the tree, if a tree root is broken or uprooted, then the tree will die. A dead tree cannot bear fruit. If generational curses are broken or uprooted from a family's bloodline; Satan, nor his demonic helpers, will have the authority to create chaos in that particular lineage.

Williams acknowledges that a generational curse is a defilement passed down from one generation to the other. He said that if parents are involved in the occult, they will become polluted and unclean, opening doors to generational curses. Not only are curses handed down from parents, but demons also move down with these curses as well. Remember, the devil lives in one of the heavens according to Daniel 10:13. In fact, God did not strip Satan of his power, God denied Satan of his privileges.[3]

Jones said generational curses can be recognized by patterns that may occur in a family. For example, if the mother, uncle, or aunt of the same family never got married, but had a child or children out of wedlock; that cycle will be passed down and their children may also have children out of wedlock.[4]

McKinney believes that generational curses are the manifestation of poor choices, ungodly circumstances, bad habits, and their environment. These curses follow members of a specific lineage.[5]

I agree with McKinney. When I reflect on certain individuals in our communities, who had a fortune and valuable assets; many of them made bad investments or gambled their money away. They are not as wealthy today, as they were back then because they lost almost everything they had. I do believe that those individuals lived to regret the poor choices that they made.

There are also individuals known to us, who practiced some unhealthy habits for most of their lives. Smoking and abusing alcohol or drugs were the most common habits among them. Unfortunately, many of them developed serious health issues such as lung cancer, cirrhosis of the liver, and respiratory complications.

The reality of generational curses is also evident in various environments. There are certain subdivisions and "ghetto" areas in our communities, which seems to have a dark cloud hanging over them. They are tinted with gang violence, drug houses, joblessness, and other serious social ills. Certain areas are so dangerous, that individuals avoid these areas for fear of their lives and safety. This is a prime example of a demonic-infested environment; these vicious cycles will continue if those generational curses are not broken.

Adams articulates, "According to The Gospel Coalition: A generational curse describes the cumulative effect on a person or things that their ancestors did, believed, or practiced in the past, and a consequence of an ancestor's actions, beliefs, and sins being passed down. Our families' history and baggage impact who we are as people, whether we like it or not. You may consider your family a blessing or consider them a burden, because of the long history of negative traits they've passed down."[6]

Hanegraaff verifies that "A generational curse is believed to be passed down from one generation to another due to rebellion against God. If your family line is marked by divorce, incest, poverty, anger, or other ungodly patterns, you're likely under a generational curse. The Bible says that these curses are tied to choices. Deuteronomy 30:19 says we can either choose life and blessing or death and cursing. Our families have the greatest influence on our development, including the development of our patterns of sin. Some people even assert that generational curses are passed down along generational lines. This belief comes from Old Testament passages, which say that God punishes the children and their children, for the sins of the fathers to the third and fourth generations (Exodus 34:7)."[7]

Bucher concludes, "Generational curses are inherited from behaviors that trickle-down one generation after another, or they can be habits and strongholds, we ourselves fall into and struggle to stumble out of. Pornography, alcoholism, eating disorders, drug addiction, sexual abuse, and adultery. All of these categorically sinful habits can be considered generational curses. When we acquire a sinful habitat belief that negatively affects our lives or those around us, this is known as a generational curse."[8]

Bucher referred to generational curses as strongholds and sinful behaviors which negatively affect individuals' lives.

---

*What are strongholds? A stronghold is anything that has power over an individual. According to the scriptures, human beings are powerless against strongholds; however, they can be broken from over the lives of individuals.*

---

If strongholds are not broken, they can leave an individual feeling or thinking that he or she has developed a life of his or her own. Strongholds can also leave individuals in a gutter of depression, recurring unbelief, or consistently bad-tempered.

Brown and Yoder explain, "Curses can be inherited, they are passed down from generation to generation. The sins of our forefathers can have a devastating effect on our lives. People fight, they hate, and they feud. Such behavior often results in a curse being placed on a family unit or the whole family line. When they place a curse on a family, they are sure to include all the descendants in the curse. Their desire is to destroy the whole family line, not just an individual. In families where various forms of mental illness or specific physical illnesses have been passed down through the generation, this is often the case."[9]

Hanegraaff acknowledges that generational curses come from the Old Testament which says, God punishes the children and their children for the sins of the fathers, to the third and fourth generations. This trend of thought can be debatable, but we know that no sin goes unpunished.

Adams said that our family's history and baggage impact who we are as people, whether we like it or not. Yes! Generational curses can be handed down in bloodlines, whether we like it or not.

Brown and Yoder explained that when a curse is placed on an individual, the person sending the curse is sure to include their children and children's children as well. Their desire is to destroy the whole family, not just one individual. Nevertheless, God has given the body of Christ the power and authority, to destroy the works of the enemy.

Unfortunately, some individuals feel that they must resort to dabbling in the dark arts to hurt others, rather than working out their differences. The Bible tells us what will happen to individuals who dabble in the dark arts.

> *"And the soul that turneth after such as have familiar spirits, and after wizards, to go a whoring after them, I will even set my face against that soul and will cut him off from among his people." ~Leviticus 20:6*

According to the scriptures, dabbling in the dark arts will bring curses to an individual. God said that He will set face against that person and will cut them off from among his people. Whatever choices we make, their results will be passed down in our bloodline.

# Chapter Two

## Do Generational Curses Really Exist?

*"These were nobler than those in
Thessalonica, in that they received the word
with all readiness of mind, and searched the
scriptures daily, whether those things were
so." ~Acts 17:11*

In the book of 2 Kings chapter 5, a detailed account is given of how generational curses do exist. It also validates how individuals can bring curses upon themselves. Those curses can be handed down from one generation to the other. Naaman, captain of the host of the King of Syria, had leprosy; He sent a message to the Prophet Elisha in the hope of receiving his healing. In return, he received a message from the prophet instructing him to wash in the Jordan River.

After Naaman followed the instructions of the prophet Elisha and washed in the Jordan River seven times; leprosy left his body. Naaman was extremely grateful to the prophet, so he tried to show his gratitude by giving him a talent of silver and two changes of garments. The prophet refused to take the gifts from Naaman and went on his way. Gehazi, Elisha's servant, allowed greed and dishonesty to fill his heart. He followed Naaman and told him that his master had sent him to receive the gifts, which were offered earlier. Naaman was thankful for his healing; therefore, he gave the gifts to Gehazi. Before Gehazi returned to the Prophet Elisha, he knew what Gehazi had done. According to the scriptures:

> *"… he said unto him, Went not mine heart*
> *with thee when the man turned again from*
> *his chariot to meet thee? Is it a time to*
> *receive money, and to receive garments, and*
> *olive yards, and vineyards, and sheep, and*
> *oxen, and menservants, and maidservants?*
> *The leprosy therefore of Naaman shall*
> *cleave unto thee, and unto thy seed forever.*
> *And he went out from his presence a leper as*
> *white as snow." ~2 Kings 5:26-27*

Since Gehazi received the talent of silver and two changes of garments, he also received leprosy which was on Naaman's body. Gehazi's lies, greed, and deception; are key examples of how individuals can cause a curse to be placed on themselves. Also, how doors are opened for curses to be passed down through their bloodline. The scriptures are clear that curses do exist, and they can be handed down to future generations.

## A Generational Curse or Not?

When Jesus was on this earth, persons living in that part of the world believed that certain infirmities were the result of generational curses. St. John chapter 9 gives an interesting account of a man who was blind from birth. As Jesus and His disciples passed by and saw the blind man, the disciples wanted to know why this man was blind. St John's Gospel states:

> *"And his disciples asked him, saying, Master,*
> *who did sin, this man, or his parents, that he*
> *was born blind?" Jesus answered, neither*

*hath this man sinned, nor his parents: but*
*that the works of God should be made*
*manifest in him." ~John. 9:2-3*

The mere fact that the disciples asked Jesus who sinned, suggests that there was a possibility that a generational curse could have been passed down to this blind man.

Kail said, "The sins of parents do have an adverse effect on their children and open the door for similar patterns of sin. When parents who are meant to provide spiritual protection for their children walk in iniquity, idolatry, and sin; children are left more vulnerable to the enemy's work. As the sin of Adam and Eve passed on to their offspring, so our sinful tendencies can pass on to our offspring."[1]

I agree with Kail. This is true and should be a revelation to all. God has given parents and guardians a mandate to protect their children physically, mentally, and spiritually.

*"My people are destroyed for lack of*
*knowledge: because thou hast rejected*
*knowledge, I will also reject thee, that thou*
*shalt be no priest to me: seeing thou hast*
*forgotten the law of thy God, I will also*
*forget thy children." ~Hosea 4:6*

Adams explains, "An example of a generational curse is divorce. Your parents grew up in homes with divorced parents, so they both lacked a clear picture of what a healthy relationship looks like. With this negative example, your parents developed unhealthy relationship habits and passed those on to you. You might be afraid of commitment because you are afraid of passing down the same trauma, or pain that you experienced as a child to your own children. And this fear of commitment may prevent you from experiencing the gift and freedom found in authentic love."[2]

Unfortunately, many individuals do not realize that generational curses are attached to them or their families. When individuals are faced with certain issues in their lives, many of them believe that those misfortunes, setbacks, and disappointments are normal occurrences. They assume that these incidents happen to everyone, at some point in their lives.

---

*They accept these curses as a part of life and try to personally deal with them themselves, not realizing that their children and children's children, will face those same issues if this vicious cycle is not broken.*

---

Nori encourages individuals to live a generational lifestyle. He said, "The direction you travel today will pave the way for your children's journey tomorrow."[3]

Both Brown and Yoder declare, "Many people vow to God that if He heals them, they will serve Him for the rest of their lives. Then, when they are well, they forget about their vow. This sort of sin brings the person under a curse from God."[4]

Ewing explains that generational curses can be obtained from property. He reminds us of Hiel the Bethelite, who was not aware of the curse levied on Jericho by Joshua. Hiel decided to redevelop the city of Jericho, as he was laying the foundation to reconstruct Jericho; his first son by the name of Abiram died. Further, as he was about to set up the gates of Jericho, his youngest son by the name of Segub died. According to I Kings 16:34, this was a result of what Joshua had spoken over Jericho 600 years earlier.

Also, in Deuteronomy chapter 7, God specifically told the Children of Israel just before they traveled into Canaan, not to marry the inhabitants of that land. More importantly, to destroy their images, jewelry, altars, and groves; He said to burn them with fire. Their land was cursed, as a result, whatever came from that land was automatically cursed and would be passed on to whoever associated with the inhabitants, and the objects of that land.[5]

The information from the various sources is incredibly convincing; generational curses are very real and can raise havoc on individuals and their families. The story of Hiel the Bethelite, who tried to redevelop the cursed land, was heartbreaking. Even though he was not aware that the land had been cursed, ignorance could not be used as an excuse; consequently, he lost both of his sons as a result. This story warns persons who purchase a piece of land that is cursed, that curse will be passed on to them.

If you plan to purchase a piece of land, save yourself headaches and grief; do your homework, and research the history of that piece of land. Ask questions about the land and its previous owners; neighbors nearby should be able to provide you with vital information on the land before you purchase it.

It was surprising to find out that general curses can be attached to family heirlooms and other valuables as well. Therefore, individuals must be careful when receiving gifts, especially family heirlooms. It would be wise for persons to find out the history of such gifts, as curses can be attached to them and unknowingly passed down to the person receiving them.

*"Whoso boasteth himself of a false gift is like clouds and wind without rain." ~Proverbs 25:14*

Persons must pray for clarity concerning land acquired, rented, or being considered for purchase, as generational curses may cause hindrances and other challenges in their lives. If a piece of land is already purchased, and the individual suspect a curse is attached to it, then he or she must seek help from their religious leaders in breaking alleged curses off their land.

> *"That at the name of Jesus every knee should bow, of things in heaven, and things in earth, and things under the earth; And that every tongue should confess that Jesus Christ is Lord, to the glory of God the Father."*
> *~Philippians 2:10-11*

# Chapter Three

## Examples Of Generational Curses In The Bible

*"Thy word have I hid in mine heart, that I
might not sin against thee." ~Psalm 119:11*

According to the book of Genesis chapter 1, when God created the earth, He saw that it was good. After Adam and Eve sinned in the Garden Eastward in Eden, sin changed the course of nature.

The serpent was the first of God's creations to be cursed. From the beginning of time, curses were passed down from generation to generation. Moses states the following:

*"...the LORD God said unto the serpent
because thou hast done this, thou art cursed
above all cattle, and above every beast of the
field; upon thy belly shalt thou go, and dust
shalt thou eat all the days of thy life."
~Genesis. 3:14.*

Every snake in this world moves on its belly because a curse was handed down to all snakes. That curse is still enforced today and will continue as long as this world exists.

Unfortunately, Eve was disobedient to God. She ate the forbidden fruit and then gave it to her husband to eat as well. Because of her disobedience, God told Eve that she would bring forth children in sorrow. That sorrow was handed down from Eve to every woman throughout the generations. When the time comes for a woman to bring forth a child into this world, as her body prepares itself for childbirth, she will encounter a very painful experience. Today, that sorrowful experience is known as "labor". In the writings of Moses God said:

> *"Unto the woman ... I will greatly multiply*
> *thy sorrow and thy conception; in sorrow,*
> *thou shalt bring forth children; and thy*
> *desire shall be to thy husband, and he shall*
> *rule over thee." ~Genesis. 3:16*

God gave Adam dominion and authority over the earth but when Adam sinned, he gave that dominion and authority over to Satan. Sin entered the world and so did curses which ushered in sicknesses, diseases, fear, and death. Moses explains what God said to Adam:

> *"...because thou hast hearkened unto the*
> *voice of thy wife, and hast eaten of the tree,*
> *of which I commanded thee, saying, Thou*
> *shalt not eat of it: cursed is the ground for*
> *thy sake; in sorrow shalt thou eat of it all the*
> *days of thy life." Thorns also and thistles*
> *shall it bring forth to thee; and thou shalt*
> *eat the herb of the field." ~Genesis. 3:17-18.*

Adam's only job was to take care of the Garden, God provided everything else that was needed. Adam never had to work the ground to find food, dig for water or search for shelter. Moses maintains that God said:

> *"In the sweat of thy face shalt thou eat bread, till thou return unto the ground; for out of it wast thou taken: for dust thou art, and unto dust shalt thou return." ~Genesis. 3:19.*

Sin changed Adam's Deoxyribonucleic acid (DNA). Since he was the father of the human race, that sinful DNA was passed on to all humans. The Bible declares that sin brought on the curses of spiritual death and then physical death. Every man, woman, and child who is born into this world, will eventually die. God formed man from the dust of the ground, and one day we will all return to the ground.

When God drove Adam and Even out of the Garden Eastward of Eden, He put Cherubim's and a flaming sword which turned every way to keep them out. From that day, men had to find food, water, clothing, and shelter for themselves.

## Blessings and Curses Passed Down in Families

The book of Genesis also gives a remarkable description of how generational curses were obtained and passed down in bloodlines. They began with Noah and his children. According to the scriptures, after the flood Noah farmed, he also planted vineyards and produced wine. At some point, Noah got drunk and during this time, he was exposed but in his tent. His son Ham, saw his nakedness and told his two other brothers Shem, and Japheth what he had seen. The two brothers covered up their father so that they would not see his nakedness. After Noah became sober, he realized that his youngest son saw him naked, so he cursed Canaan, his grandson to be a servant. However, he blessed the two other sons Japheth and Shem. Moses explains that:

The scriptures made it clear that individuals can curse others, and these curses can be passed down from one generation to the other if they are not broken.

## Generational Curses Acquired and Passed Down

The story of King David is an interesting example of how generational curses can be acquired and passed down to future generations. Even though David was the King of Israel and could have chosen any woman he wanted, he desired Bathsheba, the wife of Uriah. After she became pregnant, King David tried to cover up his sins by calling Uriah from the battlefield. David sent Uriah home to his wife, hoping that he would sleep with her so that the pregnancy would be blamed on him. When that attempt failed, David had Uriah placed in the hottest section of the battle, where he knew that Uriah would certainly be killed. After the death of Uriah, God sent the Prophet Nathan to confront David about what he had done, and how it displeased Him. The book of Samuel says:

*he shall lie with thy wives in the sight of this
sun." ~2 Samuel 12:10-11.*

King David sinned and as a result, curses were spoken over him, and calamity began in his house. For example:

- Absalom commanded his servant to kill his brother Amnon, for raping their half-sister, Tamar.
- The child that Bathsheba carried for King David; God took that child in death.
- Absalom slept with several of his father's concubines.
- Absalom rose up against his father David, to take away his throne.
- Absalom stole the love of the ten tribes.
- Absalom was killed by one of his father's soldiers.

The scriptures are clear that curses of adultery, rape, death, incest, rebellion, murder and the power struggle became attached to King David. These curses were passed down throughout King David's generations.

Curses were acquired by several families in the Bible because of their bad choices and sinful behavior. Their children and future generations; inherited those curses which brought chaos to their lives. These biblical examples of generational curses are clear and very real. Therefore, individuals should be mindful that they can procure curses when their deeds are sinful. Curses will be passed down to future generations if the cycle is not broken.

# CHAPTER FOUR

## How To Recognize Generational Curses

*"But the wisdom that is from above is first
pure, then peaceable, gentle, and easy to be
intreated, full of mercy and good fruits,
without partiality, and without hypocrisy."*
*~James 3:17*

Unfortunately, generational curses are evident in our communities today. We have become so familiar with those "fall-down-drunk" alcoholics, who usually frequent the shopping areas or popular bars in the neighborhood. It has become a normal occurrence to see them comfortably sound asleep on hard concrete pavements, first thing in the morning.

It seems as if the most important thing in this world to them is, to have another drink. This is not normal behavior; especially, when women conduct themselves in this unusual manner. They can also be seen walking the streets wearing layers of soiled clothing, matted and tattered hair; raggedy shoes, or in some cases, no shoes at all. Usually, good hygiene is not evident as a part of their daily routine. However, even when some alcoholics are passed out, their bottle of booze is still safely secured in their hands. If an investigation were to be done on their family's history, it is possible that a family member was a chronic alcoholic as well.

---

*The curse of alcoholism is usually passed down through bloodlines. For some, alcoholism starts with their first drink.*

---

If an individual realizes that he or she has a powerful desire to drink booze and cannot control his or her alcohol consumption; then, drinking alcohol has power over that individual and has become a stronghold.

There is hope for combating this stronghold. Educating individuals on the short-term, and long-term effects of alcohol abuse on their bodies, can make a significant difference in the choices that they make. They can be taught how to recognize trends of alcoholism, how to make better choices regarding drinking alcohol, and that they must take responsibility for their actions and their lives. Health programs, halfway houses, and support groups are available for alcoholics as well. Unfortunately, we cannot force people to get help if they do not want it, but we can let them know that help is always available.

Many persons who find themselves in this predicament want help, but they do not know how to ask for it. Also, some people realize that they have a problem, but they are embarrassed and shy away from help. This is when mature family members and friends, should offer their support to assist these individuals through this difficult period in their lives. These persons may need to seek professional help to put them back on the right path. God has given us medical and psychiatric doctors, who studied these types of illnesses in depth. They are qualified to examine individuals and prescribe the correct medications or if needed; they can also refer individuals for the appropriate therapies and other treatments. Depending on the severity of the individual's problem, some may need to be institutionalized to assist with their recovery. Further, repentance of sins committed by their ancestors and themselves can become one of the first steps to freedom. Constant fasting and prayer by loved ones will invoke the intervention of the Holy Spirit, who will completely set them free.

Another common and visible generational curse in our communities is smoking. Sadly, some people believe that they must smoke to stay in the clique. Others would admit that their grandparents and parents smoked; they feel that following this trend would be carrying on the family's tradition. This is not a tradition; it is a curse! Smoking can cause devastating and long-term health issues in the human body.

As we view commercials on television; companies are always warning the public about cigarette smoking. If persons would only take the time to read the information on the back of a cigarette packet, they would see that there are manufacturers' warnings about the harmful effects of smoking. There is always some new disease manifesting from long-term cigarette smoking. Smoking marijuana and other harmful substances can be the result of generational curses as well.

Generational curses can deprive persons of their dignity, peace of mind, and a productive life. There are only two examples provided in this chapter on how generational curses can be recognized; unfortunately, there are many others. These cycles will continue with the younger generation because of the poor examples of older family members, the lack of knowledge, and curses were not broken. Therefore, with a higher level of education, workshops, and support groups; the younger generations can be taught about the ill effects of smoking and drug abuse; Also, how to make better choices for their future. We often wonder why so many individuals return to their unhealthy habits, after they have completed their treatments and therapies. We must realize that there is a spiritual side to generational curses as well. Only with Christian counseling, the power of prayer, fasting, and the intervention of the Holy Spirit; these curses can be completely broken, and individuals set free from bondage.

*"Pray without ceasing." ~1 Thessalonians 5:17*

Williams said generational curses can be recognized by hardships, and unusual behaviors in an individual's life, or in certain families. These events are not normal. Secular therapies or medicines cannot help or cure these individuals. However, biblical counseling would help to put them back on the road to a better quality of life.[1]

I concur with Williams. Generational curses can be recognized through the cycle of hardship and poverty. Some individuals work extremely hard throughout their lives. Yet, they seem to be "marking it on the spot" with one disaster after the other, and no progress is made. This cycle often continues with their children; only a few will go to college or make any significant contribution to society. This vicious cycle can be broken by a higher standard of education, assistance programs, a stable job, and family support. They can also be taught how to take responsibility for their lives and make wiser choices for a better future.

Jones makes it clear that generational curses are evident when there are certain negative patterns in a particular family. For example, when there is evidence of substance abuse or unmarried mothers in a family, there is a possibility that curses were passed down to that generation.[2]

We live in a world where a large sector of society believes that good morals are no longer important. Unfortunately, their examples and lifestyles teach their children the same worldview. Statistics show that a majority of teenagers engage in sexual activity before they are mature or married. This is a normal occurrence since it is accepted by our society as a normal part of life. Teenagers are encouraged to become sexually active because of what they see in entertainment houses, on social media, on television screens, and among their peers. As a result, many teenagers (unmarried/unmatured) become pregnant and have a child or children out of wedlock.

If the grandmother and the mother got pregnant and had a child or children out of wedlock, then it is highly likely that the teenagers in that family will follow their examples as well. This can be considered a generational curse; it has to be broken or this cycle will continue in their family. An unwanted pregnancy can have a devastating effect on a teenager's life because she becomes a mother. Yet mentality, she is still a child. She will not have another opportunity to enjoy her childhood, nor is she mature enough to make appropriate decisions.

Most teenagers have no idea of the responsibility that a new baby can bring to their lives. However, with a higher level of education, the assistance of youth programs, workshops, and the support from their church; teenagers will be able to take responsibility for their lives and future. They will be given the tools which will help them to avoid other unwanted pregnancies, as they become productive citizens in their homes and communities. Further, repentance of sins, continual prayer, and the intervention of the Holy Spirit, will completely break generational curses and deliver them out of bondage. They will be set free, to fulfill the purpose that God has for them on earth.

Unfortunately, there are many other strongholds such as pornography, incest, prostitution, and sex addictions, which I have not addressed in this book, but they are evident in our communities as well. These are recognizable strongholds that were passed down through bloodlines. While it is true that many teenagers follow the examples of their grandparents or parents, some are fortunate to break the cycle. They were privileged to obtain higher education and make better choices, as they became involved in community programs and prayer groups, which helped to break the cycle in their lives, and for their future generations.

According to Kail, "Similar to sinful patterns, destructive behaviors can be passed through the family line. You can often see cycles of harmful tendencies going from one generation to the next. Suicidal inclinations and self-harm can go from parents to children. Abuse of all kinds can end up passing through a family line for generations. Addictions to alcohol and drugs can run in the family. Patterns of marital breakdown and divorce can be traced through a lineage. The enemy comes to steal, kill, and destroy; he not only wants to lay hold of individuals but also to get a stronghold on whole family lines."[3]

McKinney believes that generational curses can be recognized in the form of poor-quality relationships, which are present in more than one generation.[4]

Many persons would never suspect divorce as being a generational curse. For example, two persons decide to get married, and after a while, their relationship begins to deteriorate for simple misunderstandings. Even though the couple loved each other and tried everything to make their relationship work, including secular counseling, their marriage ended in a painful divorce. They are left devastated and confused because they worked so hard to make the marriage work. After some time, they decide to remarry; unfortunately, this trend continued to the second and even third marriage, which ended in divorce as well. The curse was never broken, so it continued to manifest in their lives. Regrettably, their children and future generations will experience the same heartache.

I agree with McKinney. Poor-quality relationships can be an indicator of generational curses acquired through a bloodline if it is evident with other family members.

Unfortunately, many individuals do not take the time to find out about their family history, or the family history of their future spouse. If this couple would have made some inquiries into the family histories, it is possible that the first divorce could have been avoided. I would encourage every couple who may be considering marriage, to have some sessions of Christian counseling before they are married. Only the virtue of prayer and the intervention of the Holy Spirit can sustain a Christian marriage.

Hanegraaff affirms, "We inherit many traits and preferences from our parents that aren't always a positive influence on ourselves or others. When we acquire a sinful habit or belief, that negatively affects our lives or those around us, this is known as a generational curse. It is the shadow side of behavior passed down through the generations but is it possible to break this cycle of suffering." [5]

Hanegraaff makes an excellent point. Generational curses are recognized when individuals acquire sinful habits or beliefs, that negatively affect their lives or those around them. In addition, most people do not view poor-quality relationships as curses. They are overlooked as "just another part of life, every marriage has its problems" or "there will be misunderstandings in every relationship" because we are not perfect human beings.

Nevertheless, where curses are involved, restoration is possible. These curses can be broken from bloodlines with Christian counseling, and repentance of sins, including the sins of the ancestors. Also, by fasting, prayer, and the intervention of the Holy Spirit, who will destroy the yoke of bondage.

## Generational Curses Obtained Through Generation Properties

*"Through knowledge shall the just be delivered." ~Proverbs. 11:9*

Ewing reveals signs that may identify generational curses obtained through generation properties.

- Individuals are unable to complete projects on that property in a timely fashion.
- Usually, there is recurrent sickness among the residents of that property.
- Individuals are never able to prosper while they are on that property.
- It is virtually impossible to be married or conceive a child or children while living on that property.
- As individuals live on that property, they are afflicted with confusion and frustration.
- Usually there are strange noises in the buildings of that property, and at times, there can be strange odors as well.
- It is almost impossible to maintain any type of relationship while living on that property.
- There is always something wrong with the vehicles, machinery, and electrical equipment, as they are always breaking down or in need of repair.
- The residents of that property are vulnerable to accidents and hardship.

The signs mentioned above, are just a few of the countless issues that individuals will experience while living on a cursed property. Individuals must take a moment to pray, asking God to show them if the property they own, rent, or occupy is under a generational curse, because of the mysterious coincidences experienced there. They should also ask God to give them the wisdom that will help them to get out of the dilemma they find themselves in.[6]

Through much prayer and the intervention of the Holy Spirit, curses can be broken off properties as well.

*"If my people, which are called by my name,
shall humble themselves, and pray, and seek
my face, and turn from their wicked ways;
then will I hear from heaven, and will
forgive their sin, and will heal their land." ~
2 Chronicles 7:14*

# CHAPTER FIVE

## How Can People Live Under Generational Curses?

*"And I will bless them that bless thee, and*
*curse him that curseth thee: and in thee*
*shall all families of the earth be blessed."*
*~Genesis 12:3*

It is unfortunate that many individuals and families, who live under a generational curse or curses have no idea, nor do they understand their predicament.

Brown and Yoder explain, "A loss of knowledge of family history seriously affects our lives. We are unable to learn from the experiences of our ancestors, both good and bad. Additionally, we are unaware of the curses we have inherited through their sins. We end up walking in the same sins as our forefathers and reaping the same troubles as a result."[1]

McKinney explains that a person or family who lives under a generational curse, may have received it by accepting cursed objects. They may have been cursed by God, or by partnering with demonic entities. In addition, persons can invoke curses and other detrimental thoughts and intentions towards others.[2]

I agree with McKinney. A person who lives under a generational curse may have been cursed by God. This is quite possible. According to the Scriptures, Cain was cursed by God:

> *"And the Lord said unto Cain, Where is Abel thy brother? And he said, I know not: Am I my brother's keeper? And he said, What hast thou done? The voice of thy brother's blood crieth unto me from the ground. And now art thou cursed from the earth, which hath opened her mouth to receive thy brother's blood from thy hand; When thou tillest the ground, it shall not henceforth yield unto thee her strength; a fugitive and a vagabond shalt thou be in the earth." ~Genesis 4:9-12*

Cain had evil intentions in his heart and made terrible choices. He killed his brother Abel because of jealousy and then buried him in the ground. Therefore, he committed the first murder and performed the first funeral. When God inquired about Abel, Cain responded with a lie and without remorse. The scriptures said that Cain was a farmer, but after he committed murder, even the ground that he tilted, did not produce as before. He lived under the curses of a fugitive and a vagabond on the earth. Those curses that he acquired, were handed down to his children and future generations.

Jones makes it clear that if a family condones sin, this will open doors for them to live under generational curses. For example, if a member of a family were to steal something and the family becomes aware of the theft; instead of scolding that individual they ignore the theft, this will bring a curse on that family. When individuals in a family continue to commit ungodly acts without remorse, history will repeat itself. This happens when parents fail to teach their children honesty and the Word of God.[3]

Kail asked the question, "Have you ever wondered why some people are prone to certain sins while others are not? There are various factors that can influence this but one of them is generational curses. Sinful strongholds that are not broken, end up being passed down to the next generation. If there is a pattern of sexual sin in your family line, this may be a bigger battle for you, than for others. If one of your parents couldn't conquer uncontrollable anger, you may find that you are also prone to outbursts of rage. The same could be said of worry, greed, unbelief, pride, or other various types of sin.

*While Abraham is considered the father of the faith and had a tremendous walk with God, he committed sins and had his flaws like the rest of us.*

One time he used deception to protect himself before a king, asking Sarah to lie about being his wife and to claim only to be his sister. It is interesting that Abraham's son, Isaac, fell into this same trap. And then we know that Isaac's son, Jacob, had a problem with using deception. We can see that this pattern of sin was passed from one generation to the next."[4]

The curse of deception became attached to Abraham when he deceived King Abimelech of Gerar, by telling him that Sarah was his sister; that lie formed a curse. As a result, a curse was passed down on Abraham's seed. Jacob his grandson, was affected by this curse when he was deceived by his father-in-law, Laban. An agreement was made between Laban and Jacob that he would work for a period of seven years, to have Rachel as his wife. However, after the seven-year period expired, Jacob was misled to marry Leah, instead of Rachel. Therefore, Jacob had to work for fourteen years to marry Rachel, the woman that he loved. This story indicates that Jacob lived under a generational curse and deception was reversed on him.

Kail mentions that worry, greed, unbelief, uncontrollable anger, and pride, are all sinful strongholds, which may form into curses. Individuals who display this type of behavior, are usually accepted as they are by family, friends, and coworkers. The strongholds which are attached to them are considered their personalities. Nevertheless, there is good news! By attending regular Bible study, encouragement from the body of Christ, the support of mature family members, and Christian counseling persons can be delivered. However, through sincere repentance, prayer, fasting, and the intervention of the Holy Spirit; they will be set free.

Williams declares that a person or family can live under generational curses if they were inherited.[5]

I agree with Williams. Individuals can live under a generational curse if inherited, or they may have done something unknowingly to bring a curse upon themself. For inexperienced individuals, unpleasant events can be considered "normal occurrences" in their daily lives. Many persons were not taught about generational curses or how to recognize them. Therefore, they will not understand that these curses exist or that they can be broken.

Ewing explains that, as long as an individual is under a generational curse, there will always be patterns of weaknesses in their life. They are not their usual deficiencies, but a closer assessment will reveal that other family members have and are experiencing the same unpleasant events. individuals will also have cycles of defeat in their lives as well. However, the power of generational curses is entirely based on the lack of knowledge; they are not aware that curses exist in their family. Sorry to say, once a curse is in place on a family, the spiritual doors swing wide open, making it quite easy for anyone to place additional curses on them.[6]

According to Bucher, "Addictions and abuses can influence our behavior, but we all have the choice to shake off those chains and embrace freedom in Christ. The sins of the fathers are punished in the children by becoming the children's own sins. John Piper explains, "The hatred of God is the embodiment of what the father's problem was." The consequences of repeated sins are generational. God proclaimed to Moses that He would not leave the guilty unpunished. Why would He want His children to continue in deplorable habits that would bring them no true happiness or satisfaction?" [7]

> *The prophet Ezekiel says, "The word of the Lord came unto me again, saying, what mean ye, that ye use this proverb concerning the land of Israel, saying, The fathers have eaten sour grapes, and the children's teeth are set on edge." ~Ezekiel. 18:1-2.*

Nori explains, "Sour grapes are character qualities or inclinations toward certain behaviors, which are handed down in families through the generations. Some might call them generational sins or familiar spirits, whatever they are, our children should not have to deal with them!" [8]

Brown and Yoder said, "Curses of plagues, famine, and destruction, came upon the nation of Israel when they turned away from the Lord's instruction. The same process is happening in the lives of Christians today. We are no longer under the law as given to Moses. Jesus fulfilled the law and set us free under the new covenant in His blood. However, the spiritual principles laid down for the Children of Israel in the Old Testament, still hold true in our lives today. Demon worship and the occult are all around us, just as they were in the land of Canaan. Satan has not changed. He and his servants have just put on a veneer of sophistication to try to keep us from recognizing him."[9]

The fact that individuals can live under generational curses may be debatable. Nevertheless, Brown and Yoder make an extremely compelling case. Individuals can live under curses when they turned away from God's instructions. Spiritual principles put in place for the Children of Israel in the Old Testament, remain in effect for Christians today. For example, Malachi 3:8-9 asks the question: "Will a man rob God? Yet ye have robbed me. But ye say, wherein have we robbed thee? In tithes and offerings. You are cursed with a curse, for you have robbed me, even this whole nation." Individuals can bring curses on themselves unknowingly when they refuse to give God what is rightfully His. The tithes and offerings are prime examples that a curse can be placed upon persons because of their disobedience.

God blesses individuals with good health, gifts, and talents to secure jobs with a regular income; He only asked for ten percent of their earnings. The other ninety percent can be spent as pleased. Yet! Individuals use all of their earnings to do whatever they choose; this practice will bring a curse on them. Even though we no longer live under the laws of the Old Testament but grace, we must still keep God's commandments and be obedient to His Word.

> *"If ye love me, keep my commandments."*
> *~John 14:15*

When individuals become involved in ungodly demonic practices such as palm reading and communicating with the dead (seances), they bring curses on themselves and their future generations as well. Most persons are familiar with the story of King Saul and the witch of Endor, found in 1 Samuel 28:3–25. Participating in demonic practices did not end well for them, nor will it end well for persons who participate in these practices today. In this modern-day, Satan uses all sorts of disguises to deceive individuals unknowingly. Many of them believe that certain practices are okay because certain laws allow or encourage them. Also, their family, friends, and even church folk participate in this type of activity. This type of practice is not of God! It is demonic and should be stopped immediately.

> *"But if thine eye be evil, thy whole body shall be full of darkness. If therefore the light that is in thee be darkness, how great is that darkness! No man can serve two masters: for either he will hate the one and love the other; or else he will hold to the one, and despise the other. Ye cannot serve God and mammon." ~Matthew 6:23-24*

As Christians, when the Holy Spirit speaks to our minds, we must be receptive to His voice because He leads and guides us in all truth. Christians must also be sober-minded and vigilant. If something does not line up with the Word of God, then, it should be left alone! Bucher was convincing in her remarks that consequences for repeated sins are generational. God declared to Moses that He would not leave the guilty unpunished.

> *"God is not a man, that he should lie; neither the son of man, that he should repent: hath he said, and shall he not do it? or hath he spoken, and shall he not make it good?" ~Numbers 23:19*

Individuals may not be aware of sins that their ancestors committed, which may have caused havoc in their lives; but they have the power to change their situation and break those generational curses.

## Create A Family Tree

Creating a family tree can provide essential information about the family's struggles, setbacks, tragedies, and secrets. As the family compiles and documents their findings, individuals would soon realize that they are not alone, and other family members struggle with the same issues as they do. If the family decides to break the cycle of strange and disastrous events among them; they must come together in true repentance for sins committed by their ancestors, parents, and themselves. They must believe that God is able and just to forgive sins, no matter how big or old they may be. By developing a relationship with Christ, Christian counseling, constant fasting, prayer, and the intervention of the Holy Spirit; these curses will be broken. Individuals will be set free from bondage to pursue their dreams, live a better quality of life, and walk in their true purpose on earth.

# CHAPTER SIX

## How Can Generational Curses Influence Mental Illnesses?

*"For God hath not given us the spirit of fear;*
*but of power, and of love, and of a sound*
*mind." ~2 Timothy 1:7*

According to the scriptures, from the beginning of time God never intended for man to become sick. Consequently, all diseases, including mental illnesses, were initiated because of the "fall" of man. God warned Adam, that if he ate the fruit from the tree of knowledge of good and evil, he would "surely die". Adam ate the forbidden fruit and because of his disobedience, sicknesses, diseases, fear, and death came into the world, which was passed down to all generations.

Studies show that not every human being would become mentally ill; however, it is common among the elderly during the aging process. Many families have to learn how to cope with mental illnesses since they have loved ones, who were stricken with this disease in the prime of their lives. They must contend with the criticism, condemnation, and shame of their loved ones, who wander about in their communities acting strange, and in some cases, becoming involved in destructive behavior. As a result of their meandering, hospitalization or institutional admissions may become a regular occurrence.

If an individual presents with a form of mental illness and their family's medical history was investigated, the results may reveal that a grandparent, parent, or close relative suffered from mental illnesses as well. Mental illnesses are generational curses that were passed down through the bloodline.

Williams said that he believes generational curses can influence sicknesses or mental illnesses in families. For example, many individuals struggle with the bondage of depression which was handed down from their parents because of some defilement in the generation. He continues, I want to be clear, we were not designed to be sick; it is passed down through the bloodline. Also, according to Ezekiel 14:3-9 and Colossians 3:5-6, everyone who lives in sin is living under a curse.[1]

Jones explains that generational curses can influence sicknesses or mental illnesses because they are strongholds that need to be broken. When an individual or their family is involved in certain sins, in most cases they want to get out. Unfortunately, they do not know how to get out, so the enemy can attack them because their sin can open the doors to curses. However, I believe that individuals can develop bipolar disorder if they are under extreme stressful pressures. For example, if a husband and his wife are always arguing and fighting, the child or children would become withdrawn and may want to be someone else. I believe that they can be passed down in generations.[2]

Kail reveals, "One of the first things that doctors do is check into your family's medical history. They know that certain types of diseases tend to pass on through the family line. But what they may not recognize is that this pattern can be a spiritual problem, not just a generic one. While not every sickness is the result of a curse; sickness, disease, and mental torment are all included in the list of curses outlined in the Scriptures. Deuteronomy 28:59 speaks specifically of plagues coming upon "You and your descendants," showing the generational impact."[3]

McKinney said generational curses can influence mental illnesses in people's lives. Here are a few conditions that I believe are influenced by curses of demonic activity:

- In the case of manic depression: Curses are sent with the intention to take away personal choices, suppress, bind, and offset or depress individuals.
- Psychotic breakdowns: Are tied to people dealing with or being in partnership with demons, who are involved in authority. Individuals may hear voices that do not carry compassion and hence, begin to lose compassion for themselves and others.
- Alzheimer's disease: Tends to make individuals forget who they are, and things or events that may have happened in the past. I believe that when an individual is abused by their grandparents or parents, it can trigger this disease because it may become a part of their epigenetics, as they get older. The brain becomes fragmented, causing individuals to want to escape reality.
- Schizophrenia: This can be complex, especially when individuals experience multiple oppressions such as blockages or not tuning into reality properly. This also includes the suppression of an individual's free will. They cannot say yes, or no, to the multiple influences, good or bad.[4]

Alzheimer's and Dementia are classified as mental illnesses and are very common in our communities today.

**What is Alzheimer's?**

According to Collins English Dictionary, Alzheimer's disease is a progressive, irreversible disease characterized by degeneration of the brain cells and commonly leading to severe dementia.

**What is Dementia?**

Dementia is a disorder of the mind, affecting perception, memory, and judgment; characterized by reduced ability to remember, control muscular movements, recognize familiar objects and sounds, etc.[5]

It is heartbreaking for individuals to accept that a grandparent or parent, who was once the strong pillar of their family, is now reduced to a confused frame of skin and bone, with little, or no memory. Unfortunately, there are families in our communities who are faced with this reality every day, since they have family members who are suffering from these horrifying diseases.

Kail makes a great point when he said that mental illnesses can be a spiritual problem, not just a generic one. This reminds us that spiritual principles were put in place for the Children of Israel in the Old Testament, and they remain in effect for Christians today. Sadly, even though it was our ancestors who sinned a long time ago, generational curses can influence mental illnesses in our families today. The Gospel of St. John says:

> *"The thief cometh not, but for to steal, and to kill, and to Destroy." ~John 10:10.*

Depending on the severity of the mental illness, an individual may need to be hospitalized or institutionalized, where they can receive treatment by a professional healthcare team. Their treatment may also include medications, secular counseling, and therapies. However, God has given the body of Christ the power and authority to break the curse of mental illnesses.

Individuals must repent of their sins and the sins of their ancestors first. Christian counseling, fasting, and prayer will invoke the power and intervention of the Holy Spirit, who will set them free from mental illnesses.

## CHAPTER SEVEN

# How Generational Curses Influence Sicknesses and Diseases

*"But he was wounded for our transgressions,
he was bruised for our iniquities: the
chastisement of our peace was upon him;
and with his stripes we are healed."*
*~Isaiah 53:5*

The curses of sickness and disease are the result of sin, which were passed down through the bloodline of Adam.

Kail explains "Diseases such as cancer and heart disease; mental health, issues of depression, bipolar disorder, and anxiety; also, problems with barrenness or miscarriages, can all be passed through the family line and be inherited."[1]

Ewing indicated that he had the unfortunate experience of explaining to some Christians that, even though they have accepted the gift of salvation, this does not automatically free them from whatever curse they are operating under. While Jesus' death enables us to be free from whatever curses we are challenged with, we must now enforce the verdict of the cross.

He further explained that sickness is a curse, and ask the question: Why is it that when an individual accepts Jesus Christ as their Lord and Savior, they are not delivered from the curse of cancer or any other life-threatening disease? Even though Christ became a curse for us, which only means that through Christ's death, He took on all curses that were meant for us. Jesus Christ has now enabled us, through himself, to break curses.[2]

*According to Jones, generational curses can influence sicknesses because the fathers ate sour grapes, and the children's teeth are set on edge.*[3]

Williams maintains that we were not designed for sicknesses; however, generational curses have influenced sickness because of the defilement of our ancestors, which have been passed down through the generations.[4]

McKinney said generational curses can influence the rise of sicknesses in the same way, that children can receive some form of inoculation from their mothers. We know that the genetic material for sicknesses can be handed down from parent to child. This is observed through the process of aging such as hair loss, bones becoming brittle, etc. These changes are seen as signs of aging, yet not every person is the same. However, we can view specific sicknesses in families as generational curses, rather than just routine aging.[5]

I agree with Kail. Diseases such as cancer, heart disease, and mental illnesses are all quite common diseases that raise havoc in people's lives. Many of them are inherited and can be viewed as generational curses. Nevertheless, these curses can be broken by educating individuals on how to care for themselves and their families. Also, how to develop a positive mindset, a lifestyle change, a proper diet, and a good family support system. Further, they can be treated with prescribed medications and regular doctor check-ups. Christian counseling can help to put them on the path of recovery, but fasting and praying, will invoke the power of the Holy Spirit, who will intervene on their behalf and deliver them completely.

Unfortunately, there are many other types of sicknesses such as anorexia nervosa, obsessive-compulsive disorder, dissociative identity disorder, depression, and the list go on. These issues can also be treated by professional medical intervention and counseling. Yet, they can only be broken by the power of prayer, fasting, and the intervention of the Holy Spirit.

> *"And it shall come to pass, if thou shalt hearken diligently unto the voice of the Lord thy God, to observe and to do all his commandments which I command thee this day, that the Lord thy God will set thee on high above all nations of the earth: And all these blessings shall come on thee, and overtake thee, if thou shalt hearken unto the voice of the Lord thy God."*
>
> *~Deuteronomy 28:1-2*

Even though curses can be passed down from one generation to the other if not broken; blessings can be passed down as well.

Nori explains, "Your ancestors had crafts and skills, abilities, and talents; strength and courage that were given to them by the Lord. As you open your heart to them, everything that was good and wholesome, and powerful in your family's heritage passed into you. It has the right to pass, and you become twice the person you otherwise might have been."[6]

Generational curses can manifest at any point in a person's life, and in many forms including sicknesses and diseases. If individuals would hearken diligently unto the voice of the Lord, believe that He is whom He says He is, and be obedient to His Word, generational curses can be broken off their lives.

> *"And these signs shall follow them that*
> *believe; In my name shall they cast out*
> *devils; they shall speak with new tongues;*
> *They shall take up serpents; and if they drink*
> *any deadly thing, it shall not hurt them; they*
> *shall lay hands on the sick, and they shall*
> *recover." ~Mark. 16:17-18*

Certain curses may be deeply rooted but God has given the body of Christ the ability to recognize them, the authority to confront them, and the power to cast them out of our lives, in the name of Jesus.

# Chapter Eight

## Can Generational Curses Affect Christians?

*"And he arose out of the synagogue and entered into Simon's house. And Simon's wife's mother was taken with a great fever; and they besought him for her. And he stood over her and rebuked the fever; and it left her: and immediately she arose and ministered unto them." ~Luke 4:38-39*

It is apparent that many proclaimed Christians, do not believe that generational curses can affect them because they have surrendered their lives to Jesus Christ. They strongly believe that repentance of sins and following Christ breaks all curses. Sadly, this belief is deceptive and false. Jesus paid the price to redeem us back to the Father, only through the shedding of His blood that price could be paid. When Jesus died, He took on the curses of death, hell, and eternal separation, which was meant for the human race. Therefore, generational curses would still exist in a Christian's life if they were not broken. These curses must be dealt with by Christians, or they will continue to bring turmoil to them and their future generations.

Many Christians today have no idea what their ancestors did or participated in; especially if there were hidden family secrets. The older family members may have been sworn to secrecy in certain matters, as some secrets are hidden for a reason. In certain cases, "the family's name had to be protected" at all costs. As a result, those hidden sins may have contributed to disappointments, unhealthy relationships, drug addictions, divorce, tragedies, and short life spans.

Ewing explains that our ancestors sinned, but they are now dead, and we the existing generations are left to bear their evils, according to Lamentations 5:7. The reality of living with generational curses is not knowing what happened in the generations before us. These curses may have warranted a lifetime of struggles and adversity, for the present generation and generations to come.

Ewing warns Christians who have not dealt with the evil covenants, established by their ancestors through their practicing in, or involvement in witchcraft and similar evils. He said that more than likely, they have unknowingly accepted the baton of generational curses. Those evil contracts and agreements must be identified and broken as soon as possible.[1]

Williams stated that generational curses can affect Christians because many of them do not recognize them. They believe that the issues in their lives are normal occurrences. Most Christians are on a treadmill. Hosea 4:6 says, "My people are destroyed for lack of knowledge." Many of them do not believe in certain things, they need to be delivered!

2 Chronicles. 7:17-18 says, "And as for thee, if thou wilt walk before me, as David thy father walked, and do according to all that I have commanded thee, and shalt observe my statutes and

my Judgments: Then will I establish the throne of thy kingdom."[2]

According to Kail, "God's heart for His children is never for sickness, disease, or mental torment to afflict them: His heart is to bless and to heal, but the consequences of the "fall" and the personal sin of people, have opened the way for all types of destruction and death in the world.

---

*Being aware of the reality of generational sickness and disease, should not frighten us but equip us to receive healing; if what we are dealing with are generational words or curses."[3]*

---

McKinney agrees that generational curses can affect Christians because of their poor view of God. This can only happen when they are under a separation from the reality of God. Many of them do not know the word of God or who Christ is, so they are not living an abundant life.[4]

Hanegraaff states, "Children are punished for the sins of their fathers to the third and fourth generation (Exodus 20:5)."[5]

Brown and Yoder said, "Unfortunately, some Christians believe that they do not have to bother with curses at all. They assume that God will handle them. However, Jesus specifically told us that He has given us authority over Satan and his kingdom – Luke 10:19 "Behold, I give unto you power to tread on serpents and scorpions, and overall, the power of the enemy: and nothing shall by any means hurt you." Mark 16:17 "And these signs shall follow them that believe; In my name shall they cast out devils; they shall speak with new tongues." 2 Corinthians 7:1 "Having, therefore, these promises, dearly beloved, let us cleanse ourselves from all filthiness of the flesh and spirit, perfecting holiness in the fear of God." With authority comes responsibility, it is our responsibility to break any curse sent on us. Jesus Christ gave us the power to do so, and He expects us to use the authority given to us, in His name."[6]

Jones has a valid point. She explains that generational curses are broken through the power of the Holy Spirit, but we must ask Him to intervene in these situations so that these curses will be broken. They will not be broken by themselves.

Christians will experience sicknesses, diseases, setbacks, pain, crisis, and many other obstacles since we live in a sinful and broken world. These curses do not discriminate, they will affect anyone regardless of race, color, creed, culture, age, or religious persuasion. Therefore, our hope and trust must be in Jesus Christ and in what He did for us at Calvary. Christians must have faith in God and believe that He will deliver them from whatever the enemy has set for them.

> *"And Jesus said unto him, Go thy way; thy*
> *faith hath made thee whole." ~Mark 10:52*

Through confession of known and unknown sins, sincere repentance, fasting, much prayer, and the intervention of the Holy Spirit; every Christian can be delivered and set free from the awful effects of generational curses.

## CHAPTER NINE

## Should Generational Curses Be Taken Seriously?

*"The leprosy therefore of Naaman shall
cleave unto thee, and unto thy seed forever.
And he went out from his presence a leper as
white as snow." ~2 Kings 5:27*

Williams said, I believe some individuals feel that generational curses exist, but they do not take them seriously. They believe that they can find a way around these curses, but they must recognize these curses for what they are, and deal with them by the blood of Jesus. Persons cannot deal with an issue unless they recognize it. They believe that there is another way. Yes, individuals accept the fact that they may be living under generational curses but many of them do not care. They believe that "a pill" will solve their problems. According to Deuteronomy 28, curses can manifest under any category.[1]

Jones responded by saying no! We do not take the thought of generational curses seriously; most individuals are not educated on that subject. I would say that older people are more knowledgeable, and they take it more seriously. Only approximately 35% of the younger population believe that generational curses exist.[2]

McKinney states that some individuals take the thought of generational curses seriously. Those who believe curses exist can recognize their patterns. Some persons have no exposure to the existence of generational curses, so they see their lives as normal. I believe that if individuals are educated about these curses, and how they can affect their lives, they will use the information gained to move from under those curses.[3]

According to Bucher, "There will always be consequences for sins and disobedience. A good father disciplines His children, and so does our Father lovingly guide us, despite the painful onslaught of our bad and disobedient decisions, but we are not held accountable for someone else's sin.[4]

I agree with Butcher. God is a God of wisdom, righteousness, and truth; He will not hold us accountable for someone else's sins.

> *"And it shall come to pass, if thou shalt hearken diligently unto the voice of the Lord thy God, to observe and to do all his commandments which I command thee this day, that the Lord thy God will set thee on high above all nations of the earth: And all these blessings shall come on thee, and overtake thee, if thou shalt hearken unto the voice of the Lord thy God." ~Deuteronomy 28:1-2*

Therefore, individuals must be mindful of the things that they say and do. If an individual realizes that he or she has sinned, that person must repent. Romans 6:23 says, for the wages of sin is death. Death does not always imply that an individual will stop breathing or expire. Death can come in other forms such as unfulfilled dreams and aspirations. If individuals refuse to repent of their sins and ungodly acts, curses can be passed down to their children and future generations.

Ewing explained that he sat down with many people, who said to him, that they did not believe in generational curses. They summed curses up as a "state of mind". He continued by saying, well guess what? A particular person said this to me, their great-grandmother divorced, their grandmother divorced, their mother is divorced, and now they are divorced. I will say to you as I said to that person, "Do you still think it is a state of mind? Time waits on no man, nor does the Spirit-world wait for persons to make up their minds to decide if it exists or not. The Spirit world is coexisting with us, whether we accept it or not.[5]

I do believe that generational curses should be taken very seriously. Curses imply that there is a supernatural power, which causes unpleasant things to happen to particular generations, or the relationship between particular generations. When these curses are realized, they must be broken because:

- They will destroy an individual's life and the lives of their family.
- Individuals will never accomplish their goals in life.
- Sickness and disease will attack an individual's body and their family's as well.
- It is not God's will for us to live under a generational curse or curses.
- These curses will be passed from our generation to future generations.

According to the scriptures, God has given the body of Christ, the power, and the authority to break all curses, so that life would be more rewarding, and abundant on this earth.

# CHAPTER TEN

## Can Satan Have The Legal Rights to Humans?

*"And the Lord said, Simon, Simon, behold,
Satan hath desired to have you, that he may
sift you as wheat." ~Luke 22:31*

Many individuals, even Christians are not aware that if they live outside the will of God, they leave themselves open for Satan to claim the legal rights to them. Satan wanted to claim the legal rights to Job.

*"Then Satan answered the Lord, and said,
Doth Job fear God for nought? Hast not thou
made a hedge about him, and about his
house, and about all that he hath on every
side? thou hast blessed the work of his
hands, and his substance is increased in the
land. But put forth thine hand now, and
touch all that he hath, and he will curse thee
to thy face. And the Lord said unto Satan,
Behold, all that he hath is in thy power; only*

*upon himself put not forth thine hand. So,
Satan went forth from the presence of the
Lord." ~Job 1:9-12*

The scripture says Job was a perfect, upright man; one that feared God and avoided evil. God knew how Job would react to the crisis that was about to come upon him, even before it happened. God knows our beginning and our end. He is omniscient (all-knowing), omnipotent (all-powerful), and omnibenevolent (supremely good). God made the heavens, the earth, and everything that is in them, including man. In other words, God knows everything. He has the power to do anything He pleases. God is from everlasting to everlasting, and nothing is hidden from Him. He knew the outcome of Job's dilemma before it actually happened. Job loved God and made up his mind to trust Him, no matter what happened. Therefore, when Job's wife told him to "curse God and die", He was able to say to her, "you speak as a foolish woman". Job reminded his wife that in this life, we will receive good at the hand of God, but evil will come as well. The scriptures said, in all of Job's calamities, he did not sin with his lips. Job knew who he was in Christ and that Satan did not have the legal rights to him.

Brown and Yoder explained, "Satan can gain the legal rights to assault us, even though we personally may be unaware of this device. For example, Moses led the Children of Israel out of Egypt; they wandered in the wilderness for forty years. Moses died and the Lord placed the leadership of the Children of Israel onto Joshua. God performed a miracle and parted the Jordan River so that they could cross over. God promised Joshua and the Children of Israel that He would fight their battles for them and give them the victory, but the promise was conditional. God's condition was their obedience to His commands. Jericho fell and the city was defeated through God's miraculous power. The Lord specifically commanded the Children of Israel, not to take anything from Jericho for themselves."[1]

The story of Achan verifies how Satan can gain the legal rights that will cause chaos in individuals, families, communities, or even a nation. After the Children of Israel defeated Jericho, their next battle was to go against the small town of Ai. Joshua and the Children of Israel were shocked; when the army returned home after losing thirty-six men and were defeated. Joshua prayed to the Lord and asked why they were defeated, since God had promised to fight their battles. Joshua, nor the Children of Israel, had any idea that Achan had sinned, but God knew. When Achan sinned, that gave Satan the "legal rights" to attack the Children of Israel and defeat them, because the covenant which was made between God and them, was broken. The book of Joshua states:

*"And Joshua, and all Israel with him, took
Achan the son of Zerah, and the silver, and
the garment, and the wedge of gold, and his
sons, and his daughters, and his oxen, and
his asses, and his sheep, and his tent, and all
that he had: and they brought them unto the
valley of Achor. And Joshua said, why hast
thou troubled us? The Lord shall trouble
thee this day. And all Israel stoned him with
stones, and burned them with fire after they
had stoned them with stones."*

*~Joshua. 7:24-25.*

Since Achan sinned, the entire Nation of Israel experienced defeat. Achan's sin was revealed; therefore, He and his entire family were stoned, and all of their belongings burned. Sin was in the camp, and it had to be removed. The conditional promise made between God and the Children of Israel had to be re-established, so that God would continue to fight their battles. Also, that sin of disobedience could not remain in the camp, or it would have been handed down to future generations in the form of a curse.

> *Moses said, "See, I have set before thee this day life and good, and death and evil; I call heaven and earth to record this day against you, that I have set before you life and death, blessing and cursing: therefore, choose life, that both thou and thy seed may live."*
> *~Deuteronomy 30:15, 19.*

After reading Deuteronomy 30:15, 19; I would like to emphasize the words, "Therefore, choose life, that both thou and thy seed may live". The choices that we make and the things that we do; will affect not only us but our seed as well, which includes our children and future generations.

The scriptures make it clear that Satan can acquire the legal rights to humans through their sins, disobedience, and when they come out of the will of God.

> *"Now the serpent was more subtil than any beast of the field which the Lord God had made. And he said unto the woman, Yea, hath God said, Ye shall not eat of every tree of the garden?" ~Genesis 3:1*

Houle said, "Satan is God's enemy, but he cannot attack God directly, so he attacks those made in God's image, and dearly loved by him. Satan knows his doom is sure and wants to bring as many people down with him as he can. Satan is so skillful; he is an evil genius who leads the whole world astray.

We know how to split the atom and fly to the moon, but after thousands of years, because of Satan's influence, there is still no consensus on who God is, what he requires, or if He even exists."[2]

*"And the great dragon was cast out, that old
serpent, called the Devil, and Satan, which
deceiveth the whole world: he was cast out
into the earth, and his angels were cast out
with him." ~Revelation 12:9*

Brown and Yoder maintained that Satan could gain the legal right to assault us. That statement is true. However, Christians can prevent Satan from gaining the legal rights to them and their families, by repenting of their sins and accepting Jesus Christ as their Lord and Savior. They must take responsibility for their actions, their deeds, and their lives. Also, rely on the Holy Spirit to lead them and guide them in all truth.

*"Again, you have heard that the ancients
were told, 'You shall not make false vows,
but shall fulfill your vows to the Lord."
~Matthew 5:33*

Wows made to God must be kept, if they are broken, a curse will come upon the person who made the vow. Satan could not gain the legal rights to Job because he was a just and upright man. Therefore, Satan cannot gain the legal rights to Christians either, unless they move out of the will of God, giving him the legal rights.

# CHAPTER ELEVEN

## Can Generational Curses Be Broken?

*"And the priest shall write these curses in a book, and he shall blot them out with the bitter water." ~Numbers 5:23*

According to the scriptures, generational curses can be broken. God has already given the body of Christ the power and authority to break them.

Williams says yes, generational curses can be broken. I am a pastor, and my job is to identify these curses as I sit and pray with my congregants. It is only by the power of prayer and the intervention of the Holy Spirit, that they can be delivered. This issue has to be addressed because the devil cannot cast out the devil.[1]

Jones agrees that generational curses can be broken and states that, Jesus came to set the captive free.[2]

*"Is not this the fast that I have chosen? to lose the bands of wickedness, to undo the heavy burdens, and to let the oppressed go free, and that ye break every yoke?"*

61

McKinney agrees that generational curses can be broken but individuals must recognize them for what they are. They must be willing to take responsibility for their actions and choices. Persons must turn everything over to Christ which will bring change, in the power of the Holy Spirit.[3]

Hanegraaff explains, "Through the first Adam - all have sinned and fall short of the glory of God. (Romans 3:23). Through the second Adam - Jesus Christ - atonement is offered to all. Says Paul, Just as the result of one trespass was condemnation for all men, so also the result of one act of righteousness was justification that brings life for all men (Romans 5:18). Through no act of our own we are condemned; likewise, through no act of our own, we are saved (Romans 5:12–21).

Through the shed blood of Jesus Christ, we have a new and better covenant with God the Father. Through Jesus' blood, He forgives us our sins and delivers us from iniquity. God has redeemed us from the curses being passed on from one generation to the next. This redemption comes as we understand that the root of our problems is in the spiritual realm. As we apply God's Word and power to our lives, and we choose to walk in righteousness and obedience to God, the chains of bondage will be broken. The freedom we have longed for can become reality!"[4]

Bucher explains "Jesus has broken every curse on the cross. Our cursed chains are snapped the minute we hand them over to Him. We have to do the hard work of turning from our sinful behavior, but in Christ, we are part of a new family, God's family! The power of the cross sets us free from the curse of sin that is death. Christ came for all, and all have the opportunity to embrace freedom in Him. Generational curses are a phenomenon of human nature and learn by example and influence.

Isaac Makashinyi wrote for The Gospel Coalition: Consequences, not curses, are passed on through the generations. If we are in Christ, every curse has already been broken."[5]

*"This is my body, which is broken for you."*
*~1 Corinthians 11:2*

I agree with Isaac Makashinyi. If we are in Christ, every curse has already been broken, but this will not happen automatically. The breaking of curses is accessible to the body of Christ, but we must use the power and authority that God has given to us in His Word, to break these curses.

Every individual that is born into this world becomes captive to death, hell, and the grave. Therefore, when Jesus came, shed His blood, and gave His life for the human race; He took back the keys of death, hell, and the grave from Satan, so that we can be set free. The scriptures said, "it is appointed to man to die once" but if we die in Christ, we will rise again because the grave cannot hold us forever. When we arise from our graves, we will be with Christ throughout eternity. The power of the cross can set us free from the curse of sin, which is eternal death and separation from God. God will not force anything on us because He has given us a free will to choose eternal life or death.

*"And there was delivered unto him the book*
*of the prophet Esaias. And when he had*
*opened the book, he found the place where it*
*was written, The Spirit of the Lord is upon*
*me, because he hath anointed me to preach*
*the gospel to the poor; he hath sent me to*
*heal the brokenhearted, to preach*
*deliverance to the captives, and recovering*
*of sight to the blind, to set at liberty them*
*that are bruised, To preach the acceptable*
*year of the Lord." ~Luke 4:17-19*

Brown and Yoder state, "Scriptural record shows that God always honored such prayers of repentance and brought revival and prosperity back to the nation and people of Israel. Through these prayers of repentance and confession of the sins of the forefathers, the curses were lifted off the people and the land".[6]

According to Brown and Yoder, when the Children of Israel confessed their sins and repented; God honored their prayers and brought revival and prosperity to their nation. God wants to do the same thing for the body of Christ today; He has empowered the church to break every generational curse in their bloodlines, as He transforms their lives through the power of the Holy Spirit.

> *"I am come that they might have life, and*
> *that they might have it more abundantly."*
> *~John 10:10*

Nori conveys the story of a lonely beggar who lay drunk and shivering in the muddy slime of a drainage ditch in Peking, China. He said, "Throughout the night hours, as he grew closer to death, the beggar's plight went either unnoticed or ignored by the few passersby. Finally, as the darkness gave way to the light of dawn, a stranger saw him and reached out in compassion. After gently lifting the cold broken frame of the man out of the ditch, the stranger took him into his own home. The beggar was nursed back to health, as the compassionate stranger told him of the Savior, who had come to this world to pull lost souls out of the pit of despair and eternal darkness; a Savior who came to give abundant life. The beggar turned his life over to Jesus Christ and went on to become China's first national preacher of the gospel. One act of kindness changed the destiny of an entire family for generations to come. They were transformed from a family who bequeathed an inheritance of emptiness, into one that possessed and passed on new life and the purposes of God."[7]

The story of a lonely beggar is an important example of how generational curses can be broken. An act of kindness can cause a person's life to be changed and transformed forever. As we apply God's Word to our lives, display the attributes of Jesus Christ, and choose to walk in obedience to God's Word; curses will be broken off our lives. We will show love and kindness to others, wherever we go. Blessings will follow us and be passed down to our children and future generations.

# Chapter Twelve

## Generational Curses That Were Obliviously Accepted

*"But it shall come to pass, if thou wilt not hearken unto the voice of the Lord thy God, to observe to do all his commandments and his statutes which I command thee this day; that all these curses shall come upon thee and overtake thee." ~Deuteronomy 28:15*

St. Matthew chapter 27, gives an account of how individuals can obliviously accept curses on themselves and their future generations. According to the Gospel of St. Matthew:

*"When Pilate saw that he could prevail nothing, but that rather a tumult was made, he took water, and washed his hands before the multitude, saying, I am innocent of the blood of this just person: see ye to it. Then answered all the people, and said, His blood be on us, and our children." ~Matthew. 27:24-25*

While Jesus stood before Pilate to be judged for crimes that He did not commit, the Jews carelessly accepted curses on themselves. They said, "His blood be on us, and on our children". They had no idea of what they were doing to themselves, their children, and unborn generations. Nevertheless, this act resulted in a curse on those individuals at that time and the Nation of Israel as a whole. Since then, the Jewish people continued to suffer much persecution: they were driven from their homeland and many tragic events occurred among their people. Further, between 1939-1941, millions of Jews were killed in the Holocaust. Today, those generational curses are still evident, as the Nation of Israel continues to be hated by many persons and countries.

*"No salvation is possible until the bearer of disunion, the Jew, has been rendered powerless to harm."[1] Adolf Hitler*

In February of 2022, Russia waged war on Ukraine where many Jews still reside today. It was interesting to learn that even though Mr. Volodymyr Zelenskyy, the president of Ukraine was born in Kryvyi Rih, then the Ukrainian Soviet Socialist Republic; he was born to Jewish parents. Many Jewish people are still in Ukraine; therefore, we are encouraged to pray for the Peace of Israel.

## Generational Curses Can Attach Themselves To Land

> *"For the land is full of adulterers; for because of swearing the land mourneth; the pleasant places of the wilderness are dried up, and their course is evil, and their force is not right." ~Jeremiah 23:10*

Real estate companies and private owners sell pieces of land daily. Most potential buyers would never suspect that a piece of land has a curse attached to it. Persons should get as much history as possible, on any piece of land before they make a purchase. Generational curses which are attached to a piece of land will create havoc on the new owner. The scriptures say:

*"... the Lord spake unto Moses and unto
Aaron, saying, When ye be come into the
land of Canaan, which I give to you for a
possession, and I put the plague of leprosy in
a house of the land of your possession."*
*~Leviticus 14:33-34*

Potential buyers must be careful in purchasing previously owned houses or condominiums as well. Moses stated:

*"Then the priest shall come and look, and
behold, if the plague be spread in the house,
it is a fretting leprosy in the house; it is
unclean. And he shall break down the house,
the stones of it, and the timber thereof, and
all the morter of the house; and he shall
carry them forth out of the city into an
unclean place." ~Leviticus 33:44-45)*

## Cursed Objects and Games

Persons who use the wigi ouija board and wear zodiac paraphernalia; can innocently bring destruction to themselves and their homes. Many persons wear their zodiac rings, pendants, and signs as a fashion, or because their friends wear them. Unfortunately, they are unaware that curses are attached to them. By using those objects, or wearing the paraphernalia, they are obliviously accepting curses on themselves. Those objects and games are considered unclean things. Anything used for Satan's service is cursed and it cannot be cleansed, so it must be destroyed by fire. It is advised that persons remove demonic-infested objects and games such: as wigi ouija boards, zodiac paraphernalia, dungeons & dragons' games, and other demonic games from their homes. Do not put them in the regular garbage bin, throw them in a container and burn them up. We often wonder why there is always confusion, crisis, or sickness in our homes; even though we maintain a regular prayer life. We must understand that there is a spiritual side to all things as well. Those objects attract demonic spirits which cause chaos in persons' lives and their homes. Further, individuals should not participate in reading horoscopes or putting their trust in them to predict their future. God holds the future in His hands, and He wants His children to trust Him.

Brown and Yoder explain, "Satan wants the children! Every parent or grandparent who serves Satan or a demon god of any sort, has dedicated their children and descendants to the service of Satan. Baby dedications are performed in every church, whether Christian or non-Christian; know where and how you are dedicating your children. When a child or even an unborn offspring is dedicated to the service of Satan, demon spirits are assigned the task of ensuring that the child remains in Satan's service all of his or her life.

Once a person who has been dedicated in such a way, accepts Jesus Christ as his Lord and Savior, he effectively breaks the dedication. To the demon spirits that were assigned to ensure fulfillment of the dedication to Satan, he had become a traitor. Immediately, a curse of destruction is then activated in his life by those demons.

Once they are born again, just about everything that could go wrong in their lives do so! They feel confused and wonder why all these terrible things are happening to them. Too often they are told that it is just the persecution that is expected in the service of Christ. We are too quick to accept this. Some persecution is inevitable but frequently, the problems are due to a curse of destruction that can be broken."[2]

I agree with Brown and Yoder. Satan wants our children and our future generations. Children are innocent and vulnerable; therefore, they should be protected by their parents or guardians. Parents or guardians should always be aware of their children's friends whom they associate themselves with, what they watch on television, and their internet interactions; also, their social media activity. They must take the time to teach their children how to pray and pray with them. Also, teach them the Word of God at home and take them to Sunday school, Sabbath school, and church services regularly.

Arming our children with the Word of God will help them to make better choices and decisions, which will carry them throughout their lives. Parents should do everything within their power to break generational curses in their lives, so that curses would not follow their children and future generations. Our children are our future, and the enemy knows this, so he will do anything to destroy them. Ignorance in accepting generational curses unaware is no excuse. The Apostle Paul says:

*"Lest Satan should get an advantage of us:*
*for we are not ignorant of his devices." ~2*
*Corinthians 2:11.*

Persons must use caution and wisdom when joining organizations. They should never be too hasty in accepting things that they are not familiar with, nor should they neglect to seek counsel in matters that they may not understand. Before persons become involved in anything unfamiliar to them, they should always pray to God for wisdom and guidance. When individuals surrender their lives to Christ, the Holy Spirit will lead and guide them in all truth; so that they would not obliviously accept generational curses.

# Chapter Thirteen

## The Importance of Teaching About Generational Curses

*"And they shall teach my people the*
*difference between the holy and profane and*
*cause them to discern between the unclean*
*and the clean." ~Ezekiel 44:23*

Teachings on generational curses and how to be set free, should be a vital part of church ministry. Many families in the church experience divorce, hardships, sicknesses, crises, addictions, and many other setbacks. Sadly, they do not understand why these things are happening in their lives and the lives of their family. Some individuals are under the impression that these occurrences are "just a part of life" and they willingly accept them without question. Unfortunately, these are the manifestations of generational curses among the body of Christ.

It is heartbreaking that even though some pastors or spiritual leaders are aware of families in their congregation, who are suffering from recurrent tragedies and setbacks; they turn a blind eye and a deaf ear to their plight. They are insensitive to the struggles of their congregants, who are bombarded by the traps and sneers of Satan. This is unaccepted in the body of Christ! Leaders should never live in fear that addressing certain issues may interrupt their congregational membership. If there are issues among the congregants, and the leader has a problem in dealing with certain matters; this would be a wonderful opportunity to partner with other individuals or ministries, who are knowledgeable in these areas. Invite them to come in and speak to their congregation on pressing issues, including, generational curses. Generational curses must be dealt with in the church because they are very real. They are destroying lives, families, communities, and the church at large. Knowledge is a powerful tool that will help the body of Christ to become aware of the issues in their lives and empower them to do something about them. Leaders should never be too busy to help individuals in their congregation. They should make the time to counsel and pray with individuals and families in the church. The church should be a place of refuge, a filling station, and a hospital for the sick and broken-hearted. God has given leaders wisdom, power, and authority; to educate their congregation on how to break all curses and dismantle the enemy's destructive devices.

> *"And these words, which I command thee*
> *this day, shall be in thine heart: And thou*
> *shalt teach them diligently unto thy children,*
> *and shalt talk of them when thou sittest in*
> *thine house, and when thou walkest by the*
> *way, and when thou liest down, and when*
> *thou risest up." ~Deuteronomy 6:6-7*

Scripture admonishes pastors and spiritual leaders to preach and teach the entire Word of God because they will be held accountable for not doing so. God calls leaders to encourage the body of Christ on how to develop a relationship with Him and to maintain a strong prayer life. Also, how to invoke the presence of the Holy Spirit, who will break generational curses, freeing families, communities, and the church from bondage.

St. Matthew's Gospel says:

*"For the Son of man is come to save that which was lost. How think ye? if a man have an hundred sheep, and one of them be gone astray, doth he not leave the ninety and nine, and goeth into the mountains, and seeketh that which is gone astray? And if so be that he find it, verily I say unto you, he rejoiceth more of that sheep, than of the ninety and nine which went not astray." ~Matthew 18:11-13*

Williams says yes! It is important to teach individuals about generational curses and their deadly impact on lives. I do believe that our country would be a better place if generational curses are realized and dealt with. Also, through prayer and the power of the Holy Spirit, generational curses can be broken off individuals and families.[1]

Jones confirms the importance of teaching individuals about generational curses, and how they may affect their lives. Also, the importance of letting them know that confession, and repentance of sins is the first step in this process.[2]

McKinney agrees that it is important to teach individuals about generational curses, and their deadly impact on their lives. He said teaching should not be limited to generational curses, but all curses.[3]

Adams states, "While your family history has an effect on you, you are not bound by these generational curses. You have the choice to continue in the footsteps of your ancestors and pass on these curses to your children, or with great diligence, you can end those curses over your life and future. You get to decide if the generational curse continues or ends. There is great freedom in breaking a generational curse and creating a healthier relationship for yourself, the people you love, and the generations to follow."[4]

Ewing agrees with Hosea 4:6 which says, "My people (Pastors, Spiritual leaders, Christians, etc.) are destroyed because of a lack of knowledge." Nevertheless, there is a spiritual law of life that says, "Through knowledge shall the just (Pastors, spiritual leaders, Christians, etc.) be delivered." (Proverbs 11:9). He said, by agreeing with his teachings does not change the spiritual laws. However, pastors and spiritual leaders will be held accountable for not preaching and teaching God's Word in its entirety; this includes the knowledge and recognition of generational curses. Many leaders do not acknowledge supernatural evil and insist that their congregation remain oblivious to its existence. The result will always be devastating, as individuals will depart this life before their time. All because their leaders insist on rejecting facts, and remain ignorant to the knowledge concerning these things, which is available in the scriptures.[5]

I concur with Ewing. Leaders will be held accountable to God for not teaching and preaching the entire Word of God. Their congregation has a right to be made aware of the devastating results of generational curses. Also, as how these curses can interrupt their lives, and how they can be set free. People are dying needlessly, and before their time because of the lack of knowledge. They should be taught by their pastors or spiritual leaders about generational curses and how to break the cycle.

*"And he said unto them, This kind can come
forth by nothing, but by prayer and fasting."
~Mark 9:29*

According to the scriptures, these curses can only be broken through the acknowledgment that they exist, confession of sins, sincere repentance of sins, faith in God, the power of fasting, continuous prayer, and the intervention of the Holy Spirit.

> *"And Jesus said unto them, Because of your unbelief: for verily I say unto you, If ye have faith as a grain of mustard seed, ye shall say unto this mountain, Remove hence to yonder place; and it shall remove; and nothing shall be impossible unto you. Howbeit this kind goeth not out but by prayer and fasting."*
> *~Matthew 17:20-21*

# Chapter Fourteen

## Is It "Taboo" To Speak About Generational Curses?

*"All things are lawful for me, but all things
are not expedient: all things are lawful for
me, but all things edify not."*
*~1 Corinthians 10:23*

Usually, most individuals prefer not to engage in conversations about curses, since they believe that curses on a whole are "taboo". On the issue of generational curses, many individuals are not knowledgeable in this area, so they refuse to entertain conversations on this topic.

Jones said I believe that speaking about generational curses is taboo. This subject intimidates most pastors because they have never studied spiritual warfare. Therefore, they would not engage in conversations on this issue. Some of them are fearful because they are not knowledgeable, so they would send members of their congregation to another pastor for more insight. Many pastors never dealt with casting out demons, and they stay away from this type of ministry. Further, there are only a few pastors that I know, who would speak about generational curses, or are willing to cast out devils.[1]

Brown and Yoder explain, "Unfortunately few people today know enough about their forefathers to know what their sins were. However, their lives are affected by those sins whether they know about them or not. Christians today have lost this concept. Failure to confess and deal with the sins of the forefathers, often results in failure when attempts are made to break inherited curses. Such inherited curses can affect individuals, families, churches, cities, states and geographical regions, or nations."[2]

Williams admitted that speaking about generational curses in our society is taboo. Most of our citizens avoid speaking about this issue because they believe there is some other way of escaping from their problems. Many individuals do not believe generational curses exist, so there is nothing to discuss. We also have those people who believe that a generational curse is just another ghost story.[3]

McKinney maintains that speaking about generational curses in itself is taboo. It may or may not be taboo when discussing it with non-family members. Most people avoid the subject because it comes with shame and condemnation.[4]

I agree with McKinney. Most people do avoid the subject because it comes with shame and condemnation. Condemnation comes because people lack the knowledge and understanding of these curses. Condemnation is not of God; it is a stronghold advocated by a demonic spirit. This spirit can be broken by the power of prayer and the intervention of the Holy Spirit.

> *"Let no corrupt communication proceed out*
> *of your mouth, but that which is good to the*
> *use of edifying, that it may minister grace*
> *unto the hearers." ~Ephesians 4:29*

Hanegraaff says, "Finally while the notion of generational curses is foreign to scripture, there is a sense in which the curse of sin has been passed on from generation to generation."[5]

Ewing advises individuals to stop allowing others to convince them that they do not have to break a curse because Christ has already broken it for them. He said, you are aware that there are still curses operating in your life, even though you have been saved. He reminds individuals that they are not enforcing the verdict of the cross. Ewing encouraged individuals to execute the verdict of the cross. Decree what the cross of Calvary has enabled them to do, which they could not achieve before Christ's Crucifixion.[6]

Butcher claims, "Less taboo generational habits can be just as dangerous and entrapping.

*Laziness, gossip, self-pity, condemnation and criticism, stubbornness, and overspending can be the damaging roots of sinful strongholds.*

She continues: a wise mentor once advised me that if I was acutely bothered by a noticeable behavior in someone else, it was most likely because I struggled with a tinge of it, or possibly sat fully entangled in it myself. God alerts us in many ways! We are not to blame our parents or grandparents for our behaviors. Even if we have inherited the same tendencies, we all have the opportunity to embrace freedom in Christ."[7]

Butcher addresses laziness, gossip, self-pity, condemnation, criticism, stubbornness, and overspending as strongholds.

**How can strongholds be identified?**

Strongholds are demonic spirits that can manifest themselves in unique ways in a person's life. A stronghold of the mind is a lie, that Satan can establish in a person's thinking, and they will believe it to be true. In reality, it is a false belief.

According to the scriptures, God is omnipresent, meaning that He is everywhere at the same time. Satan cannot be everywhere at the same time. As a result, demonic spirits which are Satan's helpers, are sent out to inject lies into the minds of humans. These demonic spirits hindered individuals' grandparents, and their parents; they were passed down to hinder this generation as well because they were never broken. For example, If an individual's grandparents or parents were lazy, and not willing to work to acquire the bare necessities of life. Usually, their children will follow in the same footsteps because this is what they were taught. Sadly, the cycle of laziness will continue in that family. What does the Bible say about laziness?

*"But if any provide not for his own, and specially for those of his own house, he hath denied the faith, and is worse than an infidel." ~1 Timothy 5:8*

*Further, "For even when we were with you, this we commanded you, that if any would not work, neither should he eat." ~2 Thessalonians 3:10*

God intended for humans to work and enjoy the labor of their hands. When God created Adam, He gave him the job of tending the garden. Yes! Adam worked. If individuals are not working to support themselves and their families, the stronghold of laziness will encourage them to lie, steal and cheat to survive. Strongholds can be broken by becoming involved in workshops at church, educational seminars, making lifestyle changes, and finding a permanent job. Also, by reading and meditating on the Word of God, prayer, fasting, and relying on the Holy Spirit to lead and guide them.

Self-pity and stubbornness are also lies injected into the minds of individuals by demonic spirits. The enemy laughs at them as they walk around grumbling about their lives, so if they are advised on how to make changes, they rather remain in their pitiful state.

Condemnation and criticism are strongholds advocated by a demonic spirit as well. God wants us to live an abundant life and prosper in this world. These strongholds can be broken when individuals are obedient to the Word of God and allow the Holy Spirit to direct their lives.

*"Let no corrupt communication proceed out*
*of your mouth, but that which is good to the*
*use of edifying, that it may minister grace*
*unto the hearers." ~Ephesians 4:29*

Gossip is a common, but deadly stronghold, which has destroyed many lives, homes, and communities; it has also infiltrated the church.

**What is gossip?**

Gossip is unrestricted conversations about other people, usually involving details that are not confirmed as being true. When gossip is recognized, individuals should seek help to break this stronghold over their lives, or it will be passed down in their generations. What does the Bible say about gossip?

*"The words of a talebearer are as wounds,*
*and they go down into the innermost parts*
*of the belly." Proverbs 18:8.*

*Further, "If any man among you seem to be*
*religious, and bridleth not his tongue, but*
*deceiveth his own heart, this man's religion*
*is vain." ~James 1:26*

Individuals should research generational curses in-depth. Ask older folk direct questions regarding issues in their family; so that they would get a better understanding of the type of curses, which may have been passed down in their bloodlines. This may be uncomfortable for family members at first, but the answers received, would give them a better insight into how some of these curses came about. Also, they would be able to break the cycle off themselves, their children, and their future generations. Persons do not have to live under generational curses, no matter how long they existed, or their origin. God wants us to be happy and live a life free from bondage.

**A word of wisdom:** Do not allow "pride" or "for the sake of the family's name" to twist reality into something that is considered "taboo"; deal with all curses head-on and get rid of them permanently.

# CHAPTER FIFTEEN

## In A Nutshell

It is remarkable that with a little research, generational curses which were overlooked for decades can now be recognized among individuals, families, and communities. Even though the information provided suggests that generational curses do influence mental illness and sickness, which are found in certain families. It is agreed that these views are verifiable. Private practices, clinics, and hospitals require personal information from patients which provides a family history. This information must be submitted before patients are examined or treated by a physician, because it gives medical professionals a baseline. If certain illnesses or conditions are known to exist in certain families, medical professionals would have some idea of where to begin with their assessments.

Individuals who participated in the research of this book provided vital information that generational curses can and will affect Christians as well. Through the shed blood of Jesus, we have a better covenant with the Father. He has given us the power and authority to break these dreadful curses from over our lives, and the lives of our future generations.

Unfortunately, curses can manifest in other ways as tragedies, struggles, addictions, and countless others. Nevertheless, some individuals use the knowledge gained about generational curses, and have learned how to break them. As a result, a transformation has taken place in their lives, and they now live a more abundant life. On the other hand, others believed that curses were "a myth" and that God will take care of them. It is with a heavy heart to reveal that, sicknesses, tragedies, struggles, addictions, and other horrible events continue to exist in their lives and the lives of their family. The scripture says my people are destroyed for lack of knowledge.

---

*We wonder why so many individuals and families go through crisis after crisis; it is because they reject the knowledge of God which will set them free.*

---

The Bible reveals that Satan can have the legal rights over humans if they walk in disobedience. Many individuals prefer to "bury their heads in the sand", rather than deal with curses. Curses can destroy individuals because evil destructive spirits are attached to them. Regrettably, there are Christians, non-Christians, and religious leaders, who refuse to accept the fact that exist. Yes, curses are very real, however, they are not to be feared because God has given the body of Christ the power and authority to break them! It is so important for religious leaders, pastors, and ministers to acquire more knowledge in this area, so that they can teach individuals in their congregation about these curses. Not only will they help to deliver their congregation from bondage, but also the community and their church as well.

**How To Begin The Process Of Breaking These Curses**

Curses and strongholds will continue in bloodline because individuals continue to follow the same destructive patterns as their ancestors. A change cannot take place unless people take responsibility for their actions, make better choices, and have a positive mindset. Curses and strongholds can be broken through engaging in community programs, participating in church programs, Christian counseling, lifestyle changes, change of diet, working with professional health caregivers, and allowing medical doctors to prescribe the appropriate medications. In severe cases, individuals may have to be institutionalized for some time, to have the necessary therapies and other special treatments. These steps can put individuals back on the right path to a fulfilling life.

**To Receive Total Deliverance from Strongholds and Generational Curses**

*"But seek ye first the kingdom of God, and
his righteousness; and all these things shall
be added unto you." ~Matthew 6:33*

God wants us to have an abundant life. Therefore, through confession of sins, sincere repentance, fasting, prayer, and the intervention of the Holy Spirit; these awful curses will be broken, and individuals set free. When Jesus was on earth, He rebuked demons and cast them out of individuals; He also spread the good news of salvation. Jesus has commanded us to do the same thing today. Yes! Generational curses do exist, but God has given the body of Christ the power and authority to break them from over their lives and the lives of others.

# CHAPTER SIXTEEN

## A Prayer to Break Generational Curses

*"Be careful for nothing; but in everything by*
*prayer and supplication with thanksgiving*
*let your requests be made known unto God."*
*~Philippians 4:6*

Father in heaven, the one true and triune God, I know that You created the heavens and the earth. You made everything that is in them, including me. I know that I live in a broken and sinful world. Because of the "fall" of man; curses, fear, sickness, diseases, and death came into the world, and we were eternally separated from you. Father, I thank You that Your Word said, I can come boldly to the throne of grace, that I may obtain mercy and find grace to help in time of need. Lord, I thank You for sending Your only Son Jesus, who shed His blood to pay the price for my sins and redeem me back to You. I believe that You can crush my enemy and sustain me, even in unbearable circumstances. I repent of every sin that my forefathers may have committed which caused curses to be passed down in my bloodline. I ask for Your forgiveness on their behalf, in the mighty name of Jesus. Lord, I also acknowledge and repent of the sins that I have committed, knowingly and unknowingly. I ask You to forgive me, in the mighty name of Jesus. O Lord break every generational curse that has been handed down through my bloodline, and set me free from every chain of bondage, in Jesus' name. I thank You for Your forgiveness and the free gift of salvation. I thank You for the indwelling of Your Holy Spirit, who will lead and guide me in all truth. I glorify Your Holy and Precious Name! Father, You are the way, the truth, and the life, the creator and author of my faith. You are mighty to save, faithful, and abundant in love for Your children. Thank You for embracing me, even when I thought that generational curses and sins would surely overwhelm me. Protect me from the tendencies and strongholds of sin that I struggle with daily. Open my eyes, open my heart, open my ears, and my mind to Your Word and Your will. Help me to build my life on You as my foundation, so that I would be rooted and grounded in You. I recognize that no person, or thing, can stop the plans that You have for my life. Generational curses are no match for the power of the One True God. I thank You for hearing and answering my prayer. I praise Your Holy name! Increase my trust in You, as I become a worker for Your Kingdom on earth. In the mighty name of Jesus, I pray, Amen.

*"Therefore I say unto you, What things
soever ye desire, when ye pray, believe that
ye receive them, and ye shall have them."
~Mark 11:24*

# Notes

A Testimony

1. Smith Wigglesworth (1859-1947). A famous quote, utilized by R.T. Kendall - Holy Fire 2014.

Chapter One - What Are General Curses?

1. Collins English Dictionary: Online dictionary. © Collins 2020. Harper Collins Publishers. Wester Hill Road.

2. Jake Kail. "4 types of generational curses". 2 Aug. 2019. Public domain.

3. Wellington Williams. Personal interview. 26 Jun. 2020

4. Teresita Jones. Personal interview. 28 Oct. 2020.

5. Rudolph McKinney. Telephone interview. 30 Oct. 2020.

6. Madeline Adams. "How Generational Curses Affect My Love Life." The Source. 21 Jul. 2020. Public domain.

7. Hank Hanegraaff. "Are Generational Curses Biblical?" Christianity.com. 19 Jun. 2020. Public domain.

8. Meg Butcher. "A Powerful Prayer to Break Generational Curses." Crosswalk.com. 21 Oct. 2020. Public domain.

9. Rebecca Brown and Daniel Yoder. Unbroken Curses: Hidden source of trouble in the Christian's life. (New Kensington: Whitaker House, 1995).

Chapter Two - Do Generational Curses Really Exist?

1. Jake Kail. "4 types of generational curses". 2 Aug. 2019. Public domain.

2. Madeline Adams. "How Generational Curses Affect My Love Life." The Source. 21 Jul. 2020. Public domain.

3. Don Nori. Breaking Generational Curses. (Shippensburg: Destiny Image Publishers, Inc., 2005).

4. Rebecca Brown and Daniel Yoder. Unbroken Curses: Hidden source of trouble in the Christian's life. (New Kensington: Whitaker House, 1995).

5. Kevin Ewing. "Generational curses obtained through generation property." The Freeport News. 12 Jul. 2018. Public domain.

Chapter Three - Examples Of Generational Curses In The Bible.

Chapter Four - How To Recognize Generational Curses.

1. Wellington Williams. Personal interview. 26 Jun. 2020

2. Teresita Jones. Personal Interview. 28 Oct. 2020.

3. Jake Kail. "4 types of generational curses". 2 Aug. 2019. Public domain.

4. Rudolph McKinney. Telephone interview. 30 Oct. 2020.

5. Hank Hanegraaff "Are Generational Curses Biblical?"

Christianity.com. 19 Jun. 2020. Public domain.

6. Ewing, Kevin. "Generational curses obtained through

generation property." The Freeport News. 12 Jul. 2018. Public

domain.

Chapter Five - How Can People Live Under Generational Curses?

1. Rebecca Brown and Daniel Yoder. Unbroken Curses: Hidden source of trouble in the Christian's life. (New Kensington: Whitaker House, 1995).

2. Rudolph McKinney. Telephone interview. 30 Oct. 2020.

3. Teresita Jones. Personal Interview. 28 Oct. 2020.

4. Jake Kail. "4 types of generational curses". 2 Aug. 2019. Public domain.

5. Wellington Williams. Personal interview. 26 Jun. 2020

6. Kevin Ewing. "Generational curses obtained through generation property." The Freeport News. 1st March 2018. Public domain.

7. Meg Butcher. "A Powerful Prayer to Break Generational." 21 Oct. 2020. Public domain.

8. Don Nori. Breaking Generational Curses. (Shippensburg: Destiny Image Publishers, Inc., 2005).

9. Rebecca Brown and Daniel Yoder, Unbroken Curses: Hidden source of trouble in the Christian's life. (New Kensington: Whitaker House, 1995).

Chapter Six – How Can Generational Curses Influence Mental Illnesses?

1. Wellington Williams. Personal interview. 26 Jun. 2020

2. Teresita Jones. Personal Interview. 28 Oct. 2020.

3. Jake Kail. "4 types of generational curses". 2 Aug. 2019. Public domain.

4. Rudolph McKinney. Telephone interview. 30 Oct. 2020.

5. Collins English Dictionary: Online dictionary. © Collins 2020. Harper Collins Publishers. Wester Hill Road.

Chapter Seven - Can Generational Curses Influence Sicknesses and Diseases?

1. Jake Kail. "4 types of generational curses". 2 Aug. 2019. Public domain.

2. Kevin Ewing. "Generational curses obtained through generation property." The Freeport News. May 2, 2019. Public domain.

3. Wellington Williams. Personal interview. 26 Jun. 2020

4. Rudolph McKinney. Telephone interview. 30 Oct. 2020.

5. Don Nori. Breaking Generational Curses. (Shippensburg: Destiny Image Publishers, Inc., 2005).

Chapter Eight - Can Generational Curses Affect Christians?

1. Kevin Ewing. "Generational curses obtained through generation property." The Freeport News. May 2, 2019. Public domain.

2. Wellington Williams. Personal interview. 26 Jun. 2020

3. Jake Kail. "4 types of generational curses". 2 Aug. 2019. Public domain.

4. Rudolph McKinney. Telephone interview. 30 Oct. 2020.

5. Hank Hanegraaff. "Are Generational Curses Biblical?" Christianity.com. 19 Jun. 2020. Public domain.

6. Rebecca Brown and Daniel Yoder. Unbroken Curses: Hidden source of trouble in the Christian's life. (New Kensington: Whitaker House, 1995).

Chapter Nine - Should Generational Curses Be Taken Seriously?

1. Wellington Williams. Personal interview. 26 Jun. 2020.

2. Teresita Jones. Personal Interview. 28 Oct. 2020.

3. Rudolph McKinney. Telephone interview. 30 Oct. 2020.

4. Meg Butcher. A Powerful Prayer to Break Generational. 21 Oct. 2020. Public domain.

6. Kevin Ewing. The cures and costly consequences of ignorance. The Freeport News. 1 Mar. 2018.

Chapter Ten - Can Satan Have The Legal Rights to Humans?

1. Rebecca Brown and Daniel Yoder, Unbroken Curses: Hidden source of trouble in the Christian's life. (New Kensington: Whitaker House, 1995).

2. Shane W. Houle "Is Satan real?" Bible For The World. 26 Apr. 2021.

Chapter Eleven - Can Generational Curses Be Broken?

1. Wellington Williams. Personal interview. 26 Jun. 2020.

2. Teresita Jones. Personal Interview. 28 Oct. 2020.

3. Rudolph McKinney. Telephone interview. 30 Oct. 2020.

4. Hank Hanegraaff. Are Generational Curses Biblical? Christianity.com. 19 Jun. 2020. Public domain.

5. Meg Butcher. A Powerful Prayer to Break Generational. 21 Oct. 2020. Public domain.

6. Rebecca Brown and Daniel Yoder, Unbroken Curses: Hidden source of trouble in the Christian's life. (New Kensington: Whitaker House, 1995).

9. Don Nori. Breaking Generational Curses. (Shippensburg: Destiny Image Publishers, Inc., 2005).

Chapter Twelve - Generational Curses That Were Obliviously Accepted.

1. Adolf Hitler. The National Museum. New Orleans, The Holocaust. Public domain.

2. Rebecca Brown and Daniel Yoder, Unbroken Curses: Hidden source of trouble in the Christian's life. (New Kensington: Whitaker House, 1995).

Chapter Thirteen - The Importance of Teaching About Generational Curses

1. Wellington Williams. Personal interview. 26 Jun. 2020.

2. Teresita Jones. Personal Interview. 28 Oct. 2020.

3. Rudolph McKinney. Telephone interview. 30 Oct. 2020.

4. Madeline Adams. "How Generational Curses Affect My Love Life." The Source. 21 Jul. 2020. Public domain.

5. Kevin Ewing. "Generational curses obtained through generation property." The Freeport News. May 2, 2019. Public domain.

Chapter Fourteen - Is It "Taboo" To Speak About Generational Curses?

1. Teresita Jones. Personal Interview. 28 Oct. 2020.

2. Rebecca Brown and Daniel Yoder, Unbroken Curses: Hidden source of trouble in the Christians life. (New Kensington: Whitaker House, 1995).

3. Wellington Williams. Personal interview. 26 Jun. 2020.

4. Rudolph McKinney. Telephone interview. 30 Oct. 2020.

5. Hank Hanegraaff. Are Generational Curses Biblical? Christianity.com. 19 Jun. 2020. Public domain.

6. Kevin Ewing. "Generational curses obtained through generation property." The Freeport News. May 2, 2019. Public domain.

7. Meg Butcher. A Powerful Prayer to Break Generational. 21 Oct. 2020. Public domain.

Chapter Fifteen - In A Nutshell

Chapter Sixteen - A Prayer to Break Generational Curses

**King James Version - Old Testament Scripture Index**

2 Kings 5:26-27
Leviticus 20:6
Hosea 4:6
Proverbs 25:14
Psalm 119:11
Genesis 3:14
Genesis 3:16
Genesis 3:17-18
Genesis 3:19
Genesis 9:24-27
2 Samuel 12:10-11
Proverbs 11:9
2 Chronicles 7:14
Genesis 12:3
Genesis 4:9-12
Ezekiel 18:1-2
Numbers 23:19
Isaiah 53:5
Deuteronomy 28:1-2
2 Kings 5:27
Job 1:9-12
Joshua 7:24-25
Deuteronomy 30:15,19
Genesis 3:1
Numbers 5:23
Isaiah 58:6
Deuteronomy 28:15
Jeremiah 23:10
Leviticus 14:33-34
Leviticus 33:44-45
Ezekiel 44:23
Deuteronomy 6:6-7
Proverbs 8:8

**King James Version - New Testament Scripture Index**

3 John 2:3
Revelation 12:11
St. Mark 9:29
St. John 8:32
Acts 17:11
St. John 9:2-3
Philippians 2:10-11
James 3:17
1 Thessalonians 5:27
St. John 14:15
St. Matthew 6:23-24
2 Timothy 1:7
St. John 10:10
3 John 2
St. Mark 16:17-18
St. Luke 4:38-39
St. Mark 10:52
St. Luke 22:31
Revelation 12:9
St. Matthew 5:33
1 Corinthians 11:2
St. Luke 4:17-19
St. Matthew 27:24-25
2 Corinthians 2:11
Matthew 18:11-13
St. Mark 9:29
St. Matthew 17:20-21
1 Corinthians 10:23
Ephesians 4:29
2 Thessalonians 3:10
St. Mark 11:24
Philippians 4:6
St. Matthew 17:21
St. Matthew 6:33

# BIBLIOGRAPHY


Adams, Madeline. How Generational Curses Affect My Love Life. The Source. 21 Jul. 2020. http://www.thesource.org/post/generational-curses-affect-my-love.

Brown, Rebecca, and Daniel Yoder. Unbroken Curses: Hidden source of trouble in the Christians' life. New Kensington: Whitaker House, 1995.

Bucher, Meg. A Powerful Prayer to Break Generational Curses. Crosswalk.com. 21 Oct. 2020. http://www.crosswalk.com/faith/prayer/a-prayer-to-break-generational.

Collins English Dictionary: Online dictionary. © Collins 2020. Harper Collins Publishers. Wester Hill Road.

http://www.collinsdictionary.com/dictionary/english

Ewing, Kevin. Generational curses obtained through generation property. The Freeport News. 12 Jul. 2018. Religion Section. Kevinewing@coralwave.com.

Ewing, Kevin. The cures and costly consequences of ignorance. The Freeport News. 1 Mar. 2018. Religion Section. Kevinewing@coralwave.com.

Shane W. Houle. Is Satan real? Bible For The World. 26 Apr. 2021.

Ewing, Kevin. Enforcing the verdict of the cross. The Freeport News. 2 May 2019. Religion Section. Kevinewing@coralwave.com.

Hanegraaff, Hank. Are Generational Curses Biblical? Christianity.com. 19 Jun. 2020.

http://www.christianity.com/wiki/christian-life/are-generational-curses-biblical.html.

Jones, Teresita. Personal Interview. Deborah Pople-Smith. 28 Oct. 2020.

Kail, Jake. 4 types of generational curses. Jake Kail. 2 Aug. 2019.

http://www.jakekail.com/4-types-of-generational-curses/

King James Bible Online. Standard King James Version 2020.

Nov. 2007. (Cambridge edition) http://www.kingjamesbibleonline.org.

McKinney, Rudolph. Telephone Interview. Deborah Pople-Smith. 30 Oct. 2020.

Nori, Don. Breaking Generational Curses. Shippensburg: Destiny Image Publishers, Inc., 2005.

http://www.destinyimage.com.

The National Museum. New Orleans. The Holocaust. (Pg.42) Public domain.

http://info@nationalww2museum.org – national ww2/war/articles/holocaust.org.

Williams Esq, Wellington A. Personal Interview. Deborah Pople-Smith. 26 Jun. 2020.